TROUBLED AND VULNERABLE CHILDREN:
A PRACTICAL GUIDE FOR HEADS

Shelagh Webb

Croner Publications Ltd
Croner House
London Road
Kingston upon Thames
Surrey KT2 6SR
Telephone: 0181-547 3333.

Published by
Croner Publications Ltd
Croner House
London Road
Kingston upon Thames
Surrey KT2 6SR
Telephone: 0181-547 3333

While every care has been taken
in the writing and editing of this book,
readers should be aware that only Acts of Parliament
and Statutory Instruments have the force of law,
and that only the courts can authoritatively
interpret the law.

British Library Cataloguing-in-Publication Data.
A catalogue record for this book
is available from the British Library.

ISBN 1 85524 275 3

Printed by Redwood Books, Trowbridge, Wiltshire

THE AUTHOR

SHELAGH WEBB is a writer on legal and social work aspects of education, who was formerly a teacher and later Director of the Education Social Work Service in Lewisham. She worked for over 20 years in local government in Manchester, Lambeth, Tower Hamlets and Lewisham. During this time she served on working parties for the DES/DFE, including that on Education, Disaffection and Juvenile Crime.

Currently she lectures for the London University Institute of Education, for a number of LEAs and for the London Borough's Training for Care Centre. As well as contributing to *The Head's Legal Guide*, she has written for *The Teacher's Legal Guide* and *Head Teacher's Briefing*.

Her publications include *The EWS and Educational Opportunities for All* (ILEA, 1986), a chapter in *Helping Troubled Children in Secondary Schools* (Blackwell, 1989) and articles for *The Guardian*, *The Times Educational Supplement* and the *Journal of Education Social Work*. As a Lambeth councillor, Shelagh is a spokesperson on education and she serves as governor for two special schools.

THE REVIEWERS

IMOGEN BURTON qualified as a solicitor and was admitted in 1978. She joined the College of Law in 1981 and is now a principal lecturer at the London branch, teaching family law, conveyancing and contract law. She designed the College's family law course which forms part of its new legal practice course for solicitors. Imogen is also co-author of *Family Law and Practice* (Jordans, 1994) and has given courses to schools on the Children Act 1989.

ROBERT MORRIS is a visiting senior research fellow in the Centre for Educational Policy and Management in the School of Education, the Open University. Dr Morris is also a tutor for the University's course E326 *Managing Schools: Challenge and Response*. He edited and contributed to *Education and the Law* (2nd edition, Longman, 1993).

Do You Require Additional Copies of This Book?

Additional copies at a special price of £9.95, including postage and packing, may now be ordered by telephoning our Customer Services team on 0181-547 3333. Please quote ref PJMP.

CONTENTS

SOURCES OF ADVICE, INFORMATION AND TRAINING

INTRODUCTION

Casting the mind back to when the **Education Reform Act 1988** first appeared one remembers the early concern about the future under the Act for the more vulnerable pupils and those who experience distress and hardship. How would they fare in the educational world of LMS, National Curriculum requirements and assessments, league tables and grant-maintained (GM) schools?

This book looks at the life experiences of disadvantaged children and considers the educational provision which is being made for them. It discusses ways of helping them and provides information about sources of advice and training. The list of organisations in chapter 9 gives prominence to sources of help which have local branches or which are also available outside London. The relevant legislation is reviewed and methods are suggested for making it work as well as possible for these needy children. The information in the book is addressed to all schools, including those which are grant-maintained or independent.

One of the most unfortunate consequences of the 1988 Act has been the rise in the number of such children who are failing, or being failed by, the school system. Under the pressure of the new financial arrangements many schools are increasingly unable to help, or even keep, those children who are expensive in resources and teacher time. There has been a steady rise both in the number of children permanently excluded from school and in the number of requests for statements. According to DFE figures, permanent exclusions increased from just under 3000 in 1990–91 to 3833 the following year, and according to research being carried out by Portsmouth University it looks as if the figure for only one term in 1993 was over 3600. Children with statements in mainstream schools rose by nearly 10,000 in one year.

All of this would be alarming enough if the 1988 Act were the only piece of legislation with which schools are having to grapple. However, over the last decade there has been a formidable increase in the volume of education law: the **Education Reform Act 1988** alone was followed by more than 50 sets of Regulations and Orders. To complicate things further, the **Children Act 1989** requires local authorities, including LEAs, to safeguard and promote the welfare of children who are in need.

As LEAs adjust to a changing and shrinking role, schools are facing a reduction in the advisory and support services which formerly worked with them in their efforts to help troubled and vulnerable children. What makes the situation critical is that the support services are being reduced just as the number of distressed and disturbed children in our society escalates.

It was pointed out recently in a debate in the House of Commons that up to 10% of today's children suffer a significant degree of emotional or behavioural disturbance during their childhood. There has also been a worrying rise (65% since 1985) in the number of children being educated in psychiatric wards and hospitals, according to a study published in May 1994 by the Association of Metropolitan Authorities (AMA, 1994). The study, which looked at special facilities provided by education and social services departments for the children whom schools cannot or will not accept, revealed a growing number of children for whom neither integrated nor special education can be offered.

We all understand that at some stage of our life distress may lead to ill health. What is not universally recognised is that in children the distress caused by family breakdown, abuse, lack of parental love and caring, bereavement or poverty can also lead to a failure to develop. However, at least as long ago as the 1976 Court Committee Report on Child Health Services, there was already evidence that adverse family and social environment could retard physical, emotional and intellectual growth (DoH, 1976).

All this is not to suggest that teachers should become therapists, or even that dealing with childhood stress is exclusively their responsibility. Clearly, Heads and teachers cannot on their own change the society in which their pupils live. They can make changes in their school, however, and there is ample evidence that, through their responses, schools have a much greater influence in children's lives than was at one time supposed.

The school does play a vital role in the health of all communities. It can be a power for good in the lives of children who are not otherwise experiencing much that is good or encouraging. It can provide a stable and consistent setting for at least part of a day which may hold much that is confusing, irrational, even frightening. School can be a place where achievements are recognised and praised, something which is important for us all, but much more so for children burdened by a sense of low self-esteem, inadequacy and helplessness.

School effectiveness is important for all pupils, but for those to whom life has already been cruel it becomes even more critical that the school should succeed. This book is a modest attempt to offer hard-pressed Heads and teachers some practical help in meeting the needs of their neediest children.

REFERENCES

AMA, *Special Child: Special Needs — Services for Children with Disabilities.* Association of Metropolitan Authorities, 1994.

DoH, *Fit for the Future: Report of the Committee of Enquiry into Child Health Services,* (The Court Report). HMSO, 1976.

CHAPTER 1

FAMILY DIFFICULTIES AND BEREAVEMENT

FAMILY BREAKDOWN

There can be very few classes or groups in our schools where there are no children who have experienced the trauma of parents' separation or divorce. The number of divorces in the UK has doubled since 1971: nearly a third of all marriages end in divorce. One in eight children are likely to experience divorce by the age of 10, and one in five by the age of 16.

As Heads and teachers are well aware, marital breakdown can be painful and protracted, and even when parents finally separate, children are likely to take several years to come to terms with their new situation. In one study 37% of the children involved were still moderately to severely depressed five years after the separation (Alsop and McCaffrey, 1993). Separation will frequently involve a change of home and/or school and financial anxieties: it will inevitably bring with it emotional disturbance.

For young children who have not reached a level of conceptual thinking and emotional understanding which will help them to comprehend what is happening, verbal conflict between two people they love is confusing and upsetting. It is even more frightening if the parents are also physically violent to each other.

All families are different, and so are the ways in which they break up, but whatever the circumstances of the separation, there will be a sense of loss, betrayal and anger for both parents and children. Children almost always want their parents to stay together and feel despair at their inability to influence what is happening. Their reactions and the behaviour they display in school will vary with their age and understanding.

Children's Reactions to Family Breakdown

Younger children (around five to eight years old) usually become very anxious, clinging and attention-seeking. They are frightened and often have reconciliation fantasies. The younger children are, the more likely they are to have a kind of magical, and guilt-inducing, belief that they could have done something about it. Although those in middle childhood (about nine to 12 years old) are beginning to develop a better understanding of other people's point of view, most will still think that their parents should be able to sort it out. That this does not happen produces anger towards parents, and at the same time the child's behaviour in school may become either sullen or disruptive.

Teenagers often cut off from their parents, feeling resentful about the effect on their life and perhaps their standard of living: they are more likely than younger children to express their anger and hostility and to want to talk about their feelings. They may be haunted by troubling memories of parental conflict and violence. Experiencing family breakdown, as with other traumas, can make adolescents worry about their sanity and they may need reassuring that their emotions are normal.

Since there are strong conventions in our society about being brought up in the nuclear family, a child can easily feel isolated and even ashamed about what is happening at home. The most recent Circular on sex education, 5/94 *Education Act 1993: Sex Education in Schools*, for example, says that pupils should be encouraged to appreciate the value of family life, marriage and the responsibilities of parenthood. However, the Circular goes on to warn teachers that many children come from backgrounds which do not reflect such values or experiences. Sensitivity is thus needed to avoid hurting them and their families, and to allow such children to feel a sense of worth.

Responding to Children from Separated Families

Children may feel embarrassed and become withdrawn if an adult at school tries to ask them questions which are tactlessly direct. However, it is always right to talk to the parent if a child's work, behaviour or concentration is deteriorating, or if a child seems unusually withdrawn. Such discussion is usually the best way of finding out if something is happening at home which is troubling the child.

Even GPs sometimes do not realise when a young person is suffering from depression. It should be recognised that children react strongly to loss, disappointment and change.

It is important that the child should know there are adults available who it is safe to talk to and who will listen to their fears and anxieties. The listening Head or teacher should avoid criticising either parent, however tempting it may be, yet allow the child to do so if they need to, and accept their feelings of anger.

Heads who would like to develop their skills in counselling, when faced with children coping with family discord or distressed by other experiences, will find a recently published book, *Counselling: Approaches and Issues in Education*, useful (Cowie and Pecherel, 1994).

There are ways of giving reassurance to a child. Jan Walker (1989) from the Newcastle Conciliation Project suggests that it may help a child to be told that:

– their feelings, even very angry ones, are normal and may last for some time

– their parents do still love them, even if this is not always obvious

- whatever has happened in their parents' relationship is not their fault
- although much in life may be changing some important things, like school, go on — concentrating on constants like school work can help the adjustment.

Children up to around 12 years of age may benefit from a 14-week programme, *Rainbows for All Children* (provided by the Leeds Diocesan RE Centre, see chapter 9), which is usually run in school after hours by specially trained teachers. Through games and stories the children are encouraged to discuss how it feels to live in the midst of a family which is disintegrating, or to cope with the death of a parent. Nigel Bavidge, who introduced the course to Britain, believes that it works as a peer-support group, with even very young children affirming each other and realising that what they are feeling is not abnormal. In such groups children can feel safer discussing things which when brought up at home may make parents tearful or angry.

Organisations Which Can Help Families in Crisis

Heads will find it useful to have a list of organisations that can give advice and support to families, some of which also provide useful information and training for schools (see the list at the end of this chapter and details in chapter 9).

Heads may also like to have available in school a series of leaflets from Young Minds (The National Association for Child and Family Health), which give simple and clear explanations of the causes of depression in children, and also describe the role of different services such as family therapy, child and family consultation, child psychologists and psycho-therapists. These would be helpful when trying to decide which professional group might give appropriate help for the particular difficulties the child is experiencing. There is a telephone service for teachers and parents which can provide information on support services in local areas.

LIVING WITH STEP-PARENTS

A child in a reconstituted family has had to cope with the loss of a parent and the shattering of the dream about being part of what the child may have wanted to believe was a happy family, no matter what the reality. The final decision about divorce or separation may be a turning point for the parents, but not for the children. They are not divorcing. They are having to grapple with the problem of finding a way to be loved by two parents who no longer love each other.

There are at least 900,000 children living in step-families in the UK. The stepchild is likely to feel a conflict of loyalties between the absent 'real' parent and the new step-parent. Sometimes there is a lot of coming and going between two households, which means that the child must struggle to adapt to different sets of rules and expectations, and may even feel that he or she doesn't belong anywhere anymore.

Although there may be some gains for all concerned in a reconstituted family, it is evident that the complexity of the situation will be very stressful and emotionally confusing for a child. Here again, an attentive ear from someone outside the family, such as a Head or teacher, can ease the strain.

The National Stepfamily Association, as well as offering advice, support and information to all members of step-families, will also give advice to teachers and others working with such families. Exploring Parenthood has published a helpful leaflet on *Step-parenting,* discussing both difficulties and gains. (See details in chapter 9.)

PARENTAL RESPONSIBILITY AND THE CHILDREN ACT 1989

The **Children Act 1989** is based on the belief that both parents should be involved in the upbringing of their children, and each parent is expected to behave responsibly towards the children. 'Parental responsibility' is defined in the Act as: "all the rights, duties, powers, responsibilities and authority which by law a parent of a child has in relation to the child and his property" (s.3[1]).

The emphasis on responsibility reflects present day thinking that parental power to control a child exists not for the benefit of the parent, but for the benefit of the child.

Both married parents automatically have parental responsibility, and continue to have it even after separation or divorce. An unmarried mother alone has parental responsibility, but an unmarried father may obtain it through a simple agreement (by completing a prescribed form) with the mother or through a court order. Other people, including step-parents, relatives, co-habitees and foster parents may legally acquire parental responsibility by court action. Parental responsibility continues until a child is 18 and can only be lost if the child is adopted or by the death of the parent.

The status of parents is much enhanced by the Act and although laws do not make people good parents, they do set a climate which fosters positive and creative attitudes. As Ben Whitney explains in his useful book for schools on the Act, "parents are to be taken seriously as part of the answer rather than being dismissed too readily as the cause of the problem" (Whitney, 1993).

The old-fashioned concepts of 'custody' and 'care and control' no longer apply, and children are instead 'resident' with one parent or both. 'Access' has been replaced by the term 'contact'. Before the Children Act, fathers sometimes felt that they were being allowed rather than expected to spend time with their children, which may have had a negative effect on their relationship.

COURT ORDERS WHEN VOLUNTARY ARRANGEMENTS BREAK DOWN

Parents may still use the court as a last resort if they are unable to come to voluntary agreements. In such cases the school needs to know the legal position of the child and the parents after a separation. The new s.8 orders used in these situations, replacing the power of the court to make custody and access orders, are:

(a) *residence order* — settling where and with whom a child is to live

(b) *contact order* — agreeing what visits or contact (eg by letter or telephone) the child may have with the person the child is not living with

(c) *prohibited steps order* — forbidding exercise of parental responsibility in a particular way (eg the parent is not to know where the child is living or not allowed to contact the school)

(d) *specific issue order* — directing how a specific question about the exercise of parental responsibility should be decided (eg allowing one parent to decide, against the wishes of the other parent, about the pupil changing school).

The **Children Act 1989** gives local authority departments a legal duty to work collaboratively to help all children in need, so it is right for Heads to be firm in their requests for information from social services in situations where the child is known to them. Schools should not, therefore, as has sometimes happened in the past, lack the information which would enable them to respond appropriately and sensitively to a child's situation. As the school is in daily contact with the child its role is crucial in supporting, assessing and monitoring a child's grappling with the trauma of changes in his or her family relationships.

City Technology Colleges (CTCs) and grant-maintained (GM) schools should be aware that the Secretary of State made an "authorisation" under ss.27 (inter-agency co-operation) and 47 (child protection procedures) of the **Children Act 1989** to the effect that schools in these two categories are recognised as "authorities" which the social services authority may, respectively, request to take specified action or call upon to assist.

Practical Implications for Schools of the New Definition of Parental Responsibility

The legal definition of a 'parent' for education procedures (s.114 of the **Education Act 1944**) was changed by s.3(5) of the **Children Act 1989** and now includes any person who has parental responsibility for the child *and* any person who has care of the child.

All those with parental responsibility, and any person who has care of the child, must be treated equally by schools and LEA staff, unless there are court orders limiting particular individuals' exercise of their responsibility. All are entitled, for instance, to vote in elections for parent governors, or in ballots about GM status, and to participate in assessments for special educational needs (SEN) (DES, 1991). They are also entitled to receive school reports if they request them and to be consulted about any major decisions for the child.

Heads and governors will therefore need to ensure that they keep up-to-date records of any people who come under the definition of parent and details of any s.8 orders. In fact, schools are required under the **Pupils' Registration Regulations 1956** (SI 1956 No. 357), as amended, to collect and store data about pupils' 'parents'. The best way of dealing with this is to question the person who comes in to register the pupil. Some authorities have developed a model for gathering this material. There are three main areas of information which schools will need.

1. Who has parental responsibility for the child and, if they do not live with the child, where do they live?
2. Who lives with the child and which of these people have parental responsibility for the child?
3. Are there any s.8 court orders which relate to the child?

Staffordshire has designed a detailed form for collecting such information which it sends home to every family, accompanied by explanatory leaflets (Whitney, 1993).

Naturally, this may be a painful process for some families and will require sensitive handling as there may be information, even 'family secrets', which they will not be willing to explain to the school. The education welfare officer (EWO) may be able to help here.

It should be noted that Administrative Memorandum (AM) 1/88, *Amendment of Pupils' Registration Regulations 1956: Keeping of School*

Records, points out that governing bodies are required only to take "reasonable steps" to identify parents. If parents choose not to offer information, exhaustive investigation is not required.

Having detailed records will make it easier to decide what to do if, for example, a parent of a child who is accommodated by the local authority arrives to collect the child from school instead of the foster parents, or a grandparent with a residence order for a pupil seeks permission to take the child on holiday during term time. Similarly, staff will need to know who to ask for parental permission to take a child on a school visit, or whom they should contact in case of illness.

If someone contacts a school claiming to have parental responsibility and the school is uncertain about their status the Head should consult the County or Borough Solicitor's Office.

For further details on the **Children Act 1989** and parental responsibility see *The Head's Legal Guide,* pages 3-483 to 497.

SINGLE-PARENT FAMILIES

There seems to be a distinct reluctance on the part of some people to accept that late in the twentieth century families come in all shapes and sizes. Over the last decade the number of families headed by a single-parent has increased by over 70% to 1.3 million. Lone-parent families now make up 19% of all families with children and it is estimated that about one in five children live in a single-parent family.

Despite the often-made political claim that most single-parent families are headed by unmarried women, marital breakdown is the predominant determining factor for single-parent families (about 60%). Single-parents are in reality far more likely to be divorced mothers older than 25, rather than unmarried teenagers. The International Year of the Family (IYF) noted that the proportion of births to unmarried teenage mothers actually *decreased* between 1981 and 1991 (IYF, 1994).

However, Britain does have a higher proportion of one-parent families than other countries in the European Union, and just over 10% of women between 20 and 39 are heads of single-parent households.

Single-parent Families and Education

It is often suggested that the structure of the traditional two-parent family is an important element in a child's ability to achieve in education. However, recent research suggests that poverty is the most important factor influencing academic performance and many children from lone-parent families are growing up in poverty.

Providing the economic background is the same, children with unmarried mothers or widowed parents perform identically to children with two parents, and although children of divorced or separated parents perform less well on average it is only by a few per cent (Ferri, 1976).

It was suggested to the Elton Committee that the increase in the number of single-parent families had in itself caused standards of behaviour in schools to deteriorate. However, the report concluded that the wide variety of causes for lone parenthood made it difficult to generalise, and that the quality of family relationships was a more important influence on children's behaviour than the number of parents (DES, 1989).

Helping Children from Single-parent Families

Heads and teachers are in a good position to help to redress the inequalities which may be experienced by one-parent families. A number of authors give advice on the relationship between one-parent families and schools, including Lambert and Streather (1980), Rogers (1983) and Reid (1989). Some of the items below come from these sources and most of the suggestions could be included on any list for helping the whole range of children experiencing difficulties or hardship in their family life.

1. Schools should ensure that the information on the child's home circumstances is regularly checked and updated with the parents, along with information about any s.8 orders.

2. Where a child's parents are separated but both parents are still involved, schools can help by establishing procedures for keeping both parents informed of the child's progress and of school events. It may be useful if there is a space available in the school for the parents to discuss any problems or disagreements about the child's education. If the relationship has a violent history then the school should ensure that the threatened parent's safety is protected.

3. Children and parents can often be helped to cope with stressful and hurtful situations if they feel able to confide in teachers, and assured that information given will only be passed on with their consent or where there is concern about the child's safety.

4. All the school staff need to be sensitive to significant changes in a child's behaviour or attitudes, eg temper tantrums, aggression, lack of concentration, depression, loss of appetite and absenteeism. Clearly such changes do not always relate to home circumstances.

5. It is important to try to cater for the child's practical needs, trying to ensure that they eat well, for example, and are kept busy without creating pressure.

6. Schools can help to break down the stigma felt by many single-parent families by ensuring that books portray a variety of family structures and that work in the classroom does not assume a 'nuclear' family. A booklist is available from the National Council for One Parent Families (see chapter 9 for address).

7. Information can be made available on sources of financial assistance for single-parents and on relevant organisations in the area who may provide support. This could be made available in a room for parents.

For further information and ideas on working with parents see pages 89 et seq.

Gingerbread, which has over 500 support groups nationally, and the National Council for One Parent Families are both organisations working for lone-parents and their children. *Parenting Alone*, is a helpful leaflet with advice on coping with the emotional and financial difficulties, and is published by Exploring Parenthood which also provides support groups and workshops (see chapter 9 for addresses).

The Child Support Act 1991

The Child Support Agency (CSA) was set up to implement the **Child Support Act 1991**. There have been serious concerns about the way in which some decisions have been made, further disadvantaging a number of separated parents. Although fathers who have been requested to pay maintenance have protested about unfairness in particular decisions, it has been estimated that as many as 70% of fathers still do not pay any maintenance.

It has been claimed by some that the **Child Support Act 1991** and the **Children Act 1989** have a similar emphasis in the way in which they stress parental responsibility, arguing that such responsibility is double edged. There are the rights of involvement in the child's life established by the Children Act (see page 5), but also the financial obligations which are stressed by the Child Support Act. However, the Child Support Act makes no provision for the wishes or feelings of the child to be taken into account, while the Children Act gives children a greater voice in decisions affecting them.

BEREAVEMENT AND LOSS

In Britain today, there are roughly 200,000 children under the age of 16 who have lost a parent by death: every year at least 10,000 young people lose a parent. As with family breakup, teachers can help children cope with loss by unobtrusively creating situations which allow the child to talk about it, or by encouraging the rest of the class to talk about a classmate who has died.

Bereavement of a close relative or friend is one of the most intensely painful experiences any human being can suffer, but for a child or adolescent the trauma is greater because of their stage of development.

Parents may feel that a child has 'got over it very well', but this can sometimes mean that the child is not yet dealing with the loss. Expressing grief is essential to reaching a resolution, but active grieving sometimes does not start for some time.

What Can Teachers do to Help Bereaved Pupils?

There are a number of ways teachers can help bereaved pupils, for example:

(a) risk initiating discussion about the subject — if it is hard for the teacher it is likely to be harder for the child, and avoiding the subject increases the sense of isolation

(b) communicate concern and sympathy but avoid platitudes about time being a great healer, etc

(c) remember that the child or teenager may be coping with many new responsibilities, even a quasi-parental role for younger siblings

(d) allow the child the space to grieve — permission is important — and do not exert pressure about 'getting back on your feet'

(e) be aware that young people often express grief indirectly through self-destructive behaviour — drug and alcohol abuse, truancy, eating disorders, etc

(f) if it is believed that more formal support is needed, suggest contacting a counsellor — the education welfare service, social services or a child guidance clinic may be appropriate.

Rebecca Abrams, whose own father died while she was still in school, has written a book, *When Parents Die*, which older pupils will find reassuring and supportive. During a number of years of interviewing and counselling bereaved teenagers, the author has been struck repeatedly "not only by their courage and fortitude, but also by their vulnerability and profound isolation" (Abrams, 1992).

Reactions to loss seem to be universal, but cultural practices modify the expression of grief, and may affect the likelihood of pathological grief. Anyone working with a bereaved child in a multicultural society ought to be familiar with different cultures and religions. Patsy Wagner's training pack for teachers on bereavement, published by the National Association for Pastoral Care in Education (NAPCE), includes some detailed notes on world religions and death (see chapter 9).

CRUSE, the national organisation for bereavement care, publishes helpful literature for children and their carers and provides a helpline for children and adults (see addresses in chapter 9).

CHILDREN LIVING IN POVERTY

According to official figures published in July 1994, almost a third of children in Britain are living below the poverty line. A report from the National Children's Bureau (NCB) (Bradshaw, 1990) concluded that child poverty had more than doubled in the 1980s and an earlier report (Townsend et al, 1987) showed that, while the purchasing value of the net incomes of the wealthiest 10% of the population had increased, the value of the poorest 10% had diminished.

The fact that children from low-income families are prone to low educational achievement is confirmed in a recent NCB study, which ends with a plea for "a sustained, all-round attack on child poverty and poor housing and living conditions, given that deep seated deprivation is the common thread linking poor housing, ill-health and educational disadvantage of children" (extract from *Poverty and Inequality in the UK* by V. Kumar, 1993, reproduced with permission from the National Children's Bureau). For children living in lone-parent families, for example, the crucial factor for academic achievement is the financial security of their family (see page 10).

Although teachers recognise that there is a correlation between poverty and academic achievement, and that poverty and poor housing create stress in the family, on a busy school day it is easy to feel impatient with what looks like parental disorganisation or neglect. Even on difficult days it is important to remember the conditions under which these families may live.

Living in poverty clearly intensifies the hardships faced in bringing up children. The income of those living on or below the poverty line means, quite simply, that they often cannot afford to pay for the basic material commodities and services which most people take for granted: adequate food, clothing, domestic appliances, heating, lighting, rent, etc. There are no margins for unexpected crises or for error and there are no overdraft facilities.

School Requests for Financial Help and Charges for School Activities

According to a survey by the National Confederation of Parent Teacher Associations (NCPTA) over the past five years there has been a threefold increase in the number of schools making direct requests for financial help from parents for equipment, books or teaching materials. Some schools are even attempting to raise money from parents to resource basic repairs and decorations and a few have asked for contributions to help pay teachers' salaries.

There has been a similar increase in requests for contributions to school trips and activities. Although charges for school trips are 'voluntary' many parents feel forced to pay because they, and the child, do not want to miss out or appear unable to pay.

DES Circular 2/89, *Education Reform Act 1988: Charging for School Activities*, gives good advice on the whole range of problems.

School Uniform and the Legal Position

It should be remembered that a number of families may have difficulty affording many items of school uniform. Although school rules frequently demand the wearing of uniform, as the law stands such a rule cannot be enforced. The question of compulsory uniform under the governors' new powers has not yet been tested in the courts.

The Effects of Poverty and the School Response

Living in poverty requires enormous energy. You are likely to lack the sort of helpful tools and machines that others take for granted to help with daily tasks, and there is little margin to indulge in those things which make a difficult life more bearable — a toy or book for a sick child, a night out, a holiday.

Many people on income support are in reality living even below this basic benefit level because of deductions to pay social fund loans, rent or fuel arrears, etc. Debt compounds poverty. A National Children's Home (NCH) study (NCB, 1992) found that most parents in debt suffer from depression, sleeplessness and acute anxiety, which in turn affects the lives of their children.

Clearly no individual school or teacher can resolve the social problems of poverty or unemployment. What can be done, and what can be crucial to a particular pupil, is to ensure that the school does not make decisions which may further disadvantage an already vulnerable child or family.

First and foremost teachers should avoid accepting, without reflection or challenge, orthodox assumptions about the nature of parents' child care. For example, the assumption that you need a father to make a complete family — the normal well-adjusted family has two heterosexual parents and that any deviation from that can only offer an inferior context for the child's development — or the assumption that a really loving and caring mother would not go out to work, or that the state of a child's clothing and 'forgetting' to bring requested items to school automatically says something about the parents' lack of organisation or even love.

In discussing or recording familial or parental characteristics it is wise first to reflect on the assumptions about pathology or normality on which one is making judgments about behaviour.

REFERENCES

Abrams, R, *When Parents Die*. Charles Letts, 1992.

Alsop, P and McCaffrey, T (eds), *How to Cope with Childhood Stress*. Longman, 1993.

Bradshaw, J, *Child Poverty and Deprivation in the UK*. National Children's Bureau, 1990.

Cowie, H and Pecherek, A, *Counselling: Approaches and Issues in Education*. David Fulton, 1994.

DES, Administrative Memorandum 1/88, *Amendment of Pupil's Registration Regulations 1956: Keeping of School Records*. HMSO, 1988.

DES, Circular 2/89: *Education Reform Act 1988: Charging for School Activities*. DES, 1989.

DES, *Discipline in Schools*, (The Elton Report). HMSO, 1989.

DES, *The Children Act 1989: A Guide for the Education Services*. The Open University, 1991.

DFE, Circular 5/94: *Education Act 1993: Sex Education in Schools*. DFE, 1994.

International Year of the Family, *Factsheet 5: Parents and Families*. UK Association IYF, 1994.

Kumar, V, *Poverty and Inequality in the UK*. National Children's Bureau, 1993.

Lambert, L and Streather, J, *Children in Changing Families*. National Children's Bureau, 1980.

National Children's Home, *Deep in Debt*. National Children's Bureau, 1992.

Reid, K, 'One-Parent Families, Pupils and Schools' in Reid, K (ed), *Helping Troubled Pupils in Secondary Schools*. Blackwell, 1989.

Rogers, R, *Children, Separation and Divorce: How Schools Can Help*. National Council for One Parent Families, 1983.

Townsend, P, et al, *Poverty and Labour in London*. Low Pay Unit, 1987.

Walker, J, 'Helping Pupils from Unsupportive Home Backgrounds: Divorce' in Reid, K (ed), *Helping Troubled Pupils in Secondary Schools*. Blackwell, 1989.
Whitney, B, *The Children Act and Schools*. Kogan Page, 1993.

SOURCES OF ADVICE, INFORMATION AND TRAINING

The following organisations may be useful sources of further information and advice. For addresses and information on the services available from these organisations please see chapter 9.

Advisory Centre for Education (ACE)
Asian Family Counselling Service
Child Poverty Action Group
Children's Legal Centre
The Children's Society
Citizens Advice Bureaux (CAB)
Contact-A-Family
CRUSE
Exploring Parenthood
Family Service Unit
Family Welfare Association
Gingerbread
Home Start UK
MIND
National Association for Pastoral Care in Education (NAPCE)
National Children's Bureau (NCB)
National Council for One Parent Families
National Stepfamily Association
Parentline
Rainbows for All Children
Relate
Women's Aid
Young Minds

CHAPTER 2

HOMELESS FAMILIES, TRAVELLERS AND REFUGEES

CHILDREN LIVING IN HOMELESS FAMILIES

The number of children living in accommodation for homeless families has been spiralling upwards over the last decade: a National Children's Bureau (NCB) study estimated that the number has in fact doubled in this period (Bradshaw, 1990).

According to statistics from the National Campaign for Homeless People (Shelter) (Burrows et al, 1992), during 1991/92 about 146,000 households were officially accepted as homeless by their local authority — a figure which the Secretary of State for the Environment stated had risen from 55,530 families in 1979 (Hansard, 19.10.92). At the time of writing there are about 13,000 families in bed and breakfast hotels in England and Wales.

The media tends to concentrate on stories of homelessness in London. In fact, it is now a substantial national problem. About 60% of households accepted as homeless in 1991, for example, were outside London and the south east.

Interrupted Schooling

Discontinuity in their schooling is the most serious educational disadvantage experienced by homeless children. Changing schools and adjusting to new teachers and new friends can in itself be a source of stress for children: when added to the disruption and uncertainty caused by moving 'home', it is hardly surprising that these children feel anxious and insecure.

Unless, or until, new legislation is passed, local authority housing departments are still responsible, under the **Housing Act 1985**, for finding accommodation for such families. Sometimes they offer accommodation which is outside the authority and it is a weakness in the present provisions that in such cases there is no obligation for the housing department to inform other statutory services, including education departments. Partly because of this, Her Majesty's Inspectors (HMI) found that many homeless children were not enrolled at schools and others were frequently absent (HMI, 1990).

Parents may travel long distances to try to keep their children in the school they were attending before they became homeless, but the strain and expense involved in such travel often leads to poor attendance. Trying to find a school nearer to the temporary accommodation is not always easy. However, the refusal of a school place on such a basis is unlawful. Helpful advice on this is given in DFE Circular 6/93, *Admissions to Maintained Schools*.

The HMI report stressed the importance of ensuring that the effects of open enrolment and formula funding do not discourage schools from accepting transient pupils and that each small gain in the security and confidence of these children as a stimulus to their learning is a worthwhile achievement (HMI, 1990).

Bed and breakfast hotels are drastically inadequate to meet the needs of family life. For example, many hotels insist on families leaving their rooms during the day so that mothers and younger children often have to wander the streets and spend more of their restricted resources in cafes trying to keep warm. Space to play or study is often very restricted and lack of cooking facilities — sometimes one stove for all the residents — means that families frequently rely on take-away meals. Poor diet, together with the damp, infested condition of many of the hotels, leads to high rates of child illness and further interrupted school attendance. In such grim conditions, older children may actually be kept at home to provide practical and emotional support for their parents.

How Can Schools Respond and Where Can They Get Support?

The trauma which caused the family to become homeless will have left its mark on the child, which may result in aggressive or withdrawn behaviour. Because of the lack of basic facilities, children often arrive in school in dirty clothes, tired, listless and unable to concentrate. Some schools have made particular arrangements to reassure and settle such children by, for example, pairing the child with another pupil to be a 'special friend'.

There is a strong case for arguing that homeless children should be defined as 'children in need' under the **Children Act 1989** and therefore they and their families would be entitled to services from the authority under Part III of the Act (see page 73). A Head may wish to inform the social services department about the child and request that they should be given assistance under the Act. When doing this the Head needs to be aware that it is the authority which has placed the child in 'homeless accommodation' which has the legal responsibility to make *caring* provision for the family.

The HMI report advised schools that the education welfare service (sometimes called the education social work service) can provide a valuable link with homeless families and can help them with information and welfare benefits. There are also voluntary organisations which offer help, for example drop-in centres and play facilities for pre-school children, and which will sometimes give support to individual schools. The local Council for Voluntary Services (number should be in your local telephone directory) will be able to give details.

Shelter offers direct practical help to homeless families through 28 housing aid centres across the country, and runs a free nightline telephone service for families in London. The Citizens Advice Bureaux offer advice on housing — there is a bureau in most towns and, again, they can be found in the local telephone directory. The Housing Campaign for Single People (CHAR) will give assistance to 16- and 17-year-olds, and information on how the **Children Act 1989** can be used to request housing for young people in need.

THE EDUCATION OF TRAVELLERS' CHILDREN

The HMI report on homeless children insisted that formula funding and open enrolment must not discourage schools from accepting transient pupils. This applies equally to travellers' children. After all, the legal duty for LEAs to make education available for school age children (**Education Act 1944**, as amended by the **Education Act 1980**) embraces *all* children residing in their area, whether permanently or temporarily, and thus includes the children of travellers.

The term 'traveller' covers a number of minority groups, each with their own distinctive lifestyle and traditions. Some travellers lead fully nomadic lives, others move only seasonally, while further groups may be settled more or less permanently in one place but travel long distances in their work. Gypsies form the largest group in the traveller community, a people whose cultural origins link them over a period of a thousand years to nomads of the Indian subcontinent. Then there are the Irish or Scottish tinkers who have travelled in this country for many years, new age travellers and fairground or circus families.

There is accommodation on official sites for only about 37% of the traveller population and a further 14% live on private authorised sites. Despite the **Caravan Sites Act 1968**, the rate at which local authorities have established sites has been slow: 40% of authorities have failed to achieve their targets. Many travellers, therefore, have no option but to camp illegally or by the roadside, where they may be vulnerable to eviction at any time.

School Attendance and Continuity in Education

In England there are between 12,000 and 15,000 traveller children of school age. Of those who do attend school, many only attend sporadically. Although parents generally can be prosecuted under s.199 of the **Education Act 1993** for failing to secure their children's regular attendance, s.199(6) states that the parent shall be acquitted if he or she proves:

(a) that he or she is engaged in a trade or business of such a nature as to require him or her to travel from place to place

(b) that the child has attended at a school as a registered pupil as regularly as the nature of that trade or business permits, and

(c) that the child has made at least 200 half-day attendances during the year before proceedings were instituted.

The purpose of this section in the 1993 Act is to protect traveller parents from unreasonable prosecution, given the nature of their work and way of life. It is not meant to imply that part-time education for traveller children is legally or even educationally acceptable, and parents still have a duty under s.36 of the **Education Act 1944** to ensure that children are receiving suitable education whether at school or elsewhere.

The aim should always be to assist traveller children, like all other children, to attend school as regularly and as frequently as possible. A balance has to be struck between the need for action in individual cases in the interest of the child and the adoption of a sensitive and sympathetic approach which recognises the lifestyle and cultural traditions of the family concerned (DFE, 1994).

A recent report from the West Yorkshire Travellers' Project found that increasingly traveller families see schooling as something desirable, although they are not yet convinced of the need for children to stay at school until 16. They expect boys to start work, usually with their fathers, in their early teens, and feel concerned for their children's sexual morals if they stay at school after puberty. The report is available from Save the Children.

For children from fairground families there are particular problems about establishing any sense of continuity in education. Their school year finishes by Easter, when their families leave their winter quarters. They return about six months later when the season is over, and then have to adjust all over again to the very different life of school. They may have learnt a number of social and business skills — maintaining equipment and dealing with money, for example — but some schools may not be very good at valuing family-taught skills. Showmen's families often complain that their children have a variety of skills, but that the schools only value literacy.

Supporting Travellers' Children in Schools

An early HMI discussion paper on the education of travellers' children concluded with a useful list of principles for practice, which includes encouraging receiving schools and teachers to acknowledge the distinctive features of the travelling way of life and to design programmes through which traveller pupils can reveal their strengths and in which they are not exposed without support to hostility or rejection (HMI, 1985).

One secondary school in Walsall gives the 20 children of showmen in the school study packs to take on tour with them. According to the Head, the school's commitment to these children is a question of equal opportunity, finding a way of making the curriculum accessible which fits in with their lifestyle. Gaining the trust of the children's families is crucial to the success of this 'distance learning' work.

Another example is the Devon Traveller Education Service which has a mobile classroom which visits fairs and works with the children.

The traveller community does not fit easily into administrative categories, and its needs range across a number of local government departments. Some authorities, such as Lewisham, have established a consortium of members from different departments to discuss and monitor provision.

A number of new initiatives for travelling and gypsy children have been set up under the European Federation for the Education of the Children of Occupational Travellers (EFECOT). Three of the projects are based in the UK. Two of them are preparing distance learning packs and the third has produced *Between Two Worlds*, a video with booklets for schools (see chapter 9 for address).

The HMI survey of the educational provision for traveller children in Essex concluded that the specialist service with 26 teachers, resource centres and mobile teaching units, had had considerable success in terms of improved access and school attendance by traveller children. A growing number of parents had been given confidence to send their children to school and schools were much more aware of the particular culture of traveller families (HMI, 1991).

Funding for LEAs and Schools to Provide Education for Travellers

Grants to facilitate the education of travellers and displaced persons are provided through the **Education (Grants) (Travellers and Displaced Persons) Regulations 1993** (SI 1993 No. 569). The term 'displaced person' here refers to those who for the time being are in accommodation provided for refugees or displaced persons. (Education for refugees is discussed on pages 26 et seq.)

The guidance in DFE Circular 11/92, *Education Reform Act 1988: Specific Grant for the Education of Travellers and of Displaced Persons*, suggests that the funding might be used to provide extra staff and resources including:

(a) peripatetic teachers or additional teaching and non-teaching staff in school

(b) additional specialist education welfare officers (EWOs) for liaison between families and schools, to secure admission and maintain attendance

(c) advisory teachers to work with schools, liaise with traveller families, EWOs, etc

(d) curriculum development and staff training

(e) development of distance learning techniques and outreach work with highly mobile children, including circus and fairground children.

Although the grants for the education of travellers and displaced persons are a mandatory exception from delegation under schemes of local management, LEAs may pass the grant on to schools as 'earmarked' funding. GM schools and CTCs can apply direct to the DFE for financial assistance towards meeting the needs of traveller pupils (26 LEAs and one GM school were approved for support for 1994–95, and 68 LEAs and one GM school had the continuation of existing projects approved — Hansard, 25.1.94).

THE EDUCATION OF REFUGEE CHILDREN

At present there are an estimated 22,000 refugee children in UK schools, 19,000 of them in Greater London. Refugee groups who help families are often seriously under-funded and face acute problems, particularly in tackling housing needs. Consequently, refugees are often left homeless, since the **Asylum Act 1993** removed the obligation on councils to house them while they seek Home Office permission to stay in this country.

There are organisations which will support teachers in their struggle to reach these children. Irene Aitman, of the Medical Foundation for the Care of Victims of Torture, says that a child "who has been traumatised is like a hedgehog with its prickles up", and schools can help children in "getting their prickles down". Members of the Foundation travel all over the country running training for teachers and speaking at staff meetings.

According to Sheila Melzak, child psychotherapist, "teachers have the potential of being the most facilitating people in these children's lives. One of the most therapeutic factors is being at school, making friends and feeling at home. And teachers have a pivotal role to play by creating a multi-cultural, multi-ethnic environment with a curriculum that explores things like conflict resolution — and issues such as bereavement and loss" (quoted from an article by Riva Klein, *TES*, 25.2.94). The National Association for Pastoral Care in Education training pack on *Children and Bereavement, Death and Loss*, might be helpful for teachers designing appropriate curriculum programmes.

A guide on *Integrating Refugee Children into Schools* (Melzak and Warner, 1992) from the Minority Rights Group reassures teachers that they can be usefully aware of the particular needs and difficulties of refugee children without having to take on the roles of psychotherapists or social workers. Schools can also consult other professionals if they believe this is necessary, though the reality is that teachers are likely to have far more contact with these children than other professionals.

The guide gives some reassuring advice. For many children the most helpful thing about school could be simply normal school boundaries, though success in school helps many children to cope, symbolising hope for the future.

Often refugee children have experienced terrible losses and it is sometimes easier to forget than to face up to the pain of loss. Mourning for family and friends, for their country and culture, is even harder when they don't know whether their friends or relatives have died or are not certain whether they will ever be able to return to their own country. However, children who can talk about their experiences are less likely to have emotional problems later, and a teacher can sometimes be crucial as a listener.

The Views of Refugee Children

The following are elements which Eritrean refugees found valuable and supportive in school:

(a) teachers who understood that they had come from a much more formal education system and had high expectations of work and behaviour

(b) teachers who asked them about themselves and made them feel that their past was valued, but who were sensitive in their approach, recognising that some would be able and wish to talk about their experiences whilst others would be unable to do so

(c) teachers who made some effort to include refugee children's backgrounds in the curriculum and asked them to prepare material on Eritrea for the class

(d) teachers who took racism seriously, so that pupils felt 'safe' in school, because racism was a shock for them

(e) schools which invited members of the Eritrean community to give talks and whose teachers attended special Eritrean cultural occasions.

(Melzak and Warner, 1992).

Further Sources of Help

The Refugee Council is another organisation which works with teachers in different parts of the country, and which will run INSET courses for local authorities and individual schools on request. The Council recommends that the parent and child should be interviewed via an interpreter and the child's language needs assessed. Unfortunately, in some authorities there have been cuts in interpreting services and s.11 funding (see page 30). (For further information on integrating pupils for whom English is a second language see pages 29 et seq.)

Waltham Forest is one of a number of boroughs making refugee children a priority, with two support teachers developing good practice in curriculum work, school ethos and admissions policies. They help to prepare pupils already in the schools to understand what it might mean to lose your home, toys etc and how to care for refugees arriving in the school. They find, incidentally, that many children thrive on befriending new classmates.

Funding for LEAs and Schools to Provide Education for Displaced Persons

The DFE specific grant for the education of travellers and of displaced persons defines displaced persons as those who are temporarily accommodated in a camp or establishment for refugees. The types of provision which DFE Circular 11/92 suggests may be grant-aided include:

(a) counselling and guidance on educational and career opportunities for displaced persons

(b) English language and other educational support for displaced persons.

(For further details of this funding see page 25.)

PUPILS FOR WHOM ENGLISH IS A SECOND LANGUAGE

The Commission for Racial Equality (CRE) and a number of Heads have expressed concern at the School Curriculum and Assessment Authority's (SCAA) recent decision to remove a reference in the English Curriculum Order which acknowledged the difficulties facing bilingual pupils. It is not unusual for some schools in inner city areas in different parts of the country to have a large number of children who on arrival may either speak virtually no English or have only a small amount of English.

The aim of the Home Office s.11 programme launched by the **Local Government Act 1966** was to help children whose mother tongue is not English. For the last two decades central funds have borne 75% of the cost of extra school specialists who develop the speaking, reading and writing skills of children from the New Commonwealth — the former British colonies which won independence in the latter half of this century. Last year the scope of s.11 programmes was widened in a private member's bill to include all ethnic minority children.

However, in April 1994 the programme was cut considerably and the Government contribution will be dropping to 50% by 1995/96, leaving local authorities struggling to make up these shortfalls. It is likely that this will have a serious effect not only on the education of children from ethnic minorities, but on all children in classes with them, since everyone's progress is slowed down when a teacher is coping without extra support. As an indication of the scale of the problem in some areas, 56% of Tower Hamlets' school population do not have English as a first language; in Bradford it is nearly 30% with a number of wards being over 95%.

Designing Programmes for Immigrant Pupils

One school with a large immigrant population is George Orwell in Islington, north London, which receives new immigrant pupils every week and has developed an induction programme which looks at the social and personal implications for the child, as well as the obvious academic difficulties. The school believes that the new pupil's most urgent need is to become a member of a school group which both provides the newcomer with an identity and gives value to each individual.

The programme includes giving the newcomer a special card holding information about the child's name, tutor group, etc which avoids confusion when a class teacher, dinner supervisor or anyone else speaks to the child. It is essential to remember that support staff can play an important role in providing a support network for new children (Lodge, 1992).

The recently formed National Association of Language Development in the Curriculum (NALDIC) has developed a network of UK teachers working for pupils with English as an additional language which could provide helpful support and information.

REFERENCES

Bradshaw, J, *Child Poverty and Deprivation in the UK*. National Children's Bureau, 1990.

Burrows et al, *Homes Cost Less Than Homelessness*. Shelter: National Campaign for Homeless People, 1992.

DFE, Circular 11/92: *The Education Reform Act 1988: Specific Grant for the Education of Travellers and of Displaced Persons*. DFE, 1992.

DFE, Circular 6/93: *Admissions to Maintained Schools*. DFE, 1993.

DFE, *School Attendance: Policy and Practice on Categorisation of Absence*. DFE, 1994.

Ferri, E, *Growing Up in a One-parent Family*. NCB/NFER, 1976.

HMI, *The Education of Travellers' Children*. HMSO, 1985.

HMI, *A Survey of the Education of Children Living in Temporary Accommodation*. HMSO, 1990.

HMI, *A Survey of Educational Provision for Traveller Children in Essex*. HMSO, 1991.

Lodge, C, 'Integrating New Pupils Who Speak No English' in *Pastoral Care in Education* Vol 10, No 2, 1992.

Melzak and Warner, *Integrating Refugee Children into Schools*. Minority Rights Group, 1992.

SOURCES OF ADVICE, INFORMATION AND TRAINING

The following organisations may be useful sources of further information and advice. For addresses and information on the services available from these organisations please see chapter 9.

CHAR — Housing Campaign for Single People

Citizens Advice Bureaux (CAB)

Devon Traveller Education Service

European Federation for the Education of the Children of Occupational Travellers

Medical Foundation for the Care of Victims of Torture

The Minority Rights Group

National Association for Pastoral Care in Education (NAPCE)
National Association of Language Development in the Curriculum
National Association of Teachers of Travellers
National Children's Bureau (NCB)
The Refugee Council
Shelter

CHAPTER 3

CHILD PROTECTION AND CHILDREN IN CARE

CHILD PROTECTION

Of all the children who may be suffering some form of distress, those who are, or may be, being abused are the cause of most anxiety to teachers. At any time there will be about 32,500 children on local authorities' child protection registers — this was the figure at 31 March 1993 — which is about four children per 1000. Much more worrying is the NSPCC estimate that three to four children die every week following abuse or severe neglect.

Although the school is not an investigation or intervention agency, it nevertheless does have a crucial role in recognition and referral. Statistically schools make a higher proportion of referrals to social services departments about the care of children than any other agency. Abuse and neglect are sometimes associated with poverty, but all schools need to be vigilant because the incidence of physical, sexual and emotional abuse is not confined to inner city areas or particular social and economic circumstances.

Since the late 1960s a number of reports have emphasised the role of the school in identifying possible cases of abuse. For example, the Seebohm Committee (RDHSS, 1968) stressed that the teacher is often the first to become aware that all is not well. In 1988, the Cleveland Report strongly recommended that careful consideration should be given to the working arrangements between schools, social workers, police and others (Butler-Sloss, 1988).

More recently the latest Government guide on child protection, *Working Together Under the Children Act 1989*, stated that the education service has an important part to play at the recognition and referral stage. Because of their day-to-day contact with individual children, teachers and other staff are particularly well placed to observe outward signs of abuse, changes in behaviour or failure to develop (Home Office/DoH/DES/Welsh Office, 1991).

Working Together consolidates and brings up-to-date previous guidance, including DES Circular 4/88, *Working Together for the Protection of Children from Abuse: Procedures within the education service*, by taking into account the requirements of the **Children Act 1989** and lessons learned from cases which have caused public concern.

Apart from parents, teaching staff are, after all, the group of adults with whom children spend most of their time. Teachers' understanding of child development gives them a particular expertise in recognising changes in behaviour and possible danger signals.

Communication with Parents and with Social Services

Although Heads may recognise their referral role, they may be reluctant to report their concerns about particular children. This may be because they fear that the social services department might respond in a way which would endanger their relationship with the family, or cause considerable, and perhaps unnecessary, distress. On the other hand, Heads sometimes believe that social workers are not taking their concerns seriously enough, and they may become frustrated by the apparent lack of action.

Both kinds of anxiety can be reduced if Heads are clear about where the boundaries of the school's responsibilities actually lie. The following five points may help to get things into focus.

1. *The designated teacher and school procedures*

Working Together requires schools to identify either the Head or a senior member of staff as the *designated teacher* whose role is to:

(a) co-ordinate action in the school

(b) ensure that there are clearly laid down child protection procedures — including procedures to be followed where a member of staff is alleged to have abused a child — which are in line with those of the local Area Committee for the Protection of Children (ACPC)

(c) liaise with social services and other agencies about children who may be being abused.

As a colleague with particular expertise, the designated teacher can make teaching staff less anxious by talking through concerns and helping to reach the difficult and sensitive decisions needed to ensure that the child is protected by the procedures.

All teachers and non-teaching staff, including those in GM and independent schools, should be aware of the need to alert social services, the NSPCC or the police, when they believe a child has been abused or is at risk of abuse (Home Office, DoH, DES, 1991). DES Circular 4/88 advises that if teachers see signs which cause them concern they may have the opportunity, tactfully and sympathetically, to seek information from the child. If this opportunity does not arise, or if the child's responses do not dispel suspicion, teachers should immediately make their concerns known to the designated teacher, who will then follow local procedures for reporting such cases.

It should be remembered that although it is the role of the school to be alert to possible signs of abuse and to report concerns, it is not the responsibility of school staff to make enquiries of parents or others involved. In some cases it might actually be counter-productive to do this. Investigation is the statutory responsibility of social services, the NSPCC and the police and should be left to them.

2. *Legal responsibilities to work together*

Working with social services and providing them with the necessary information is no longer a matter of good practice, but is a legal requirement under ss.27 and 47 of the **Children Act 1989** (see page 78). All Heads and teachers should ensure that they are familiar with the guide *Working Together* and that they have read carefully the section on the education service.

The fact that the guide was jointly prepared by all the departments (DoH, DES [DFE] and the Home Office) involved underlines the belief that arrangements for the protection of children from abuse, and in particular child protection conferences, can only be successful if the professional staff do all they can to work in partnership and share and exchange relevant information. The insight gained by teachers through close and continuous contact with the child can provide a conference with vital details for making an assessment of the child's circumstances.

GM schools and CTCs are also subject to the legal requirements to co-operate under ss.27 (inter-agency co-operation) and 47 (child protection) of the **Children Act 1989**. As with all other schools, GM and independent schools must be aware of the local procedures developed by the ACPC, and if they have not been contacted by the local ACPC the Head or designated teacher should make this link. Having the school procedures agreed with the ACPC is important for all schools in any case concerning child abuse, including one where a member of staff is alleged to have abused a pupil.

For a Head who is trying to persuade an apparently reluctant social worker to give serious consideration to a referral, it is useful to know that if the local authority is informed that a child may be at risk (ie is suffering or is likely to suffer significant harm) it is under a legal duty to investigate and decide whether to take action to protect the child.

3. Working in partnership with families

The **Children Act 1989** rests on the belief that the best place for children to be brought up and cared for is with their families wherever possible. As *Working Together* explains, the child protection provisions of the Act must be operated against this background of parental involvement, and the assumption in the Act of a high level of co-operation between parents and local authorities requires a concerted effort towards interdisciplinary and inter-agency working.

Schools should be aware that the Act requires social services to work wherever possible in partnership with parents in order to solve difficulties and concerns without recourse to the courts. Emergency protection orders have been cut by more than half, and the number of care orders granted dropped from 6200 to 1600 in the first year of the Act.

4. Acting in an emergency

In an emergency, if the Head is unable to contact the parents he or she might wish to agree to medical treatment for a child, or take action if there is serious concern that a child may be abused when returning home. The **Children Act 1989**, s.3(5), has clarified the *in loco parentis* role of anyone who is caring for a child, but who does not have parental responsibility, for example a Head, and such people may now "do what is reasonable in all the circumstances for the purpose of safeguarding or promoting the child's welfare". However, although s.3(5) covers emergency treatment, it is unclear whether major surgery is likewise covered (Masson and Morris, 1992).

5. The limits of confidentiality

Heads and teachers often worry about confidentiality when talking with children who are experiencing difficulties at home or who may be being abused. It should be remembered that the degree of confidentiality should be governed by the need to protect the child. When talking to a child, or interviewing anybody else offering information, it should be made clear that it may not be possible to maintain confidentiality if this would prejudice a child's welfare. Protecting the child must always overrule any consideration of confidentiality.

Keeping clear and detailed records about child abuse concerns is essential. Any comment about how an injury occurred should be recorded, quoting the words actually used, as soon as possible after the comment has been made. There is no need for Heads to worry about the accessibility of such records. The **Education (School Records) Regulations 1989** (SI 1989 No. 1261), which allow parents and older pupils access to school records, do not authorise or require the disclosure to them of any information in relation to the protection of children against abuse.

Child Protection Registers and Conferences

In each area covered by a social services department a central register must be maintained which lists all the children in the area who are considered to be suffering from, or are likely to suffer, significant harm. The purpose of the register is to provide a record of all children in the area who are currently the subject of an inter-agency protection plan, and to ensure that the plans are formally reviewed every six months.

Categories of abuse for the purpose of registration are defined in *Working Together* as:

1. *Neglect* — the persistent or severe neglect of a child, the failure to protect a child from exposure to any kind of danger (including cold or starvation) or extreme failure to carry out important aspects of care, resulting in the significant impairment of the child's health or development.

2. *Physical injury* — actual or likely physical injury to a child, or failure to prevent physical injury (or suffering) to a child including deliberate poisoning, suffocation and Münchhausen's syndrome by proxy.

3. *Sexual abuse* — actual or likely sexual exploitation of a child or adolescent. The child may be a dependent and/or developmentally immature.

4. *Emotional abuse* — actual or likely severe adverse effect on the emotional and behavioural development of a child caused by persistent or severe emotional ill-treatment or rejection. All abuse involves some

emotional ill-treatment, but this category should be used where it is the main or sole form of abuse.

It is useful to have these categories in mind when attending a child protection conference. The role of the conference is to bring together the family and the professionals and provide them with the opportunity to:

(a) share their concerns

(b) exchange relevant information

(c) analyse the degree of risk to the child, and

(d) make recomendations for action.

There are two kinds of child protection conference: the initial child protection conference and the child protection review. The terms are used to ensure clarity and to distinguish the meetings organised under the ACPC procedures from other case discussions. The conference will be convened by the agency with statutory powers (the SSD or the NSPCC) following an investigation and indication that a decision has to be made about further action under the child protection procedures.

The conference is *not* a forum for a formal decision that a particular person has abused a child — that is a matter for the courts to decide. Any decision to initiate an application for a care order is also not a matter for the conference, this decision rests with the agency with the statutory powers.

The representative from the school who is attending the conference should also be aware that the child, the parents and other carers will be invited to the conference. Clearly, there will be instances where the interests of the parents and children may conflict and in such cases the child's interest will be the priority.

Abused Children and Learning Difficulties

Abused children frequently have educational difficulties. The difficulties these children can have with learning are clearly part of the damage resulting from a drastic deficit in self-esteem, which also underlies a whole range of self-destructive behaviour. Their ability to explore the world with any confidence has been broken, if indeed it was ever allowed to develop in the first place. This helps to explain the frightening inability to think through the often dangerous consequences of their unpredictable behaviour, which schools have sometimes experienced with such children.

Proactive Role in Reducing Levels of Child Abuse

As well as adopting sound policies and procedures to help to protect children who are abused, teachers can play an educative role which should contribute significantly to reducing the future abuse of children. The aim will be to help pupils to develop relevant information, skills and attitudes, in order to resist abuse of themselves and to prepare them for the responsibilities of their adult lives (DES, 1991).

Curriculum programmes to prepare young people for both the practical and the emotional demands of parenthood are clearly important here, but the attitudes endemic in society which, some have argued, create a culture in which abuse is more likely to occur need to be addressed throughout the curriculum; for example, attitudes to women, media representations of violence and instinctive authoritarianism in adult/child relationships.

When we consider that the abusing parents of the next generation are sitting in our classrooms now, then the urgency of such debates and attempts to influence the attitudes of those future adults becomes self-evident. Any schools wishing to study this theme in more detail will find a useful stimulus to thinking in the chapters by Peter Maher in *Child Abuse: the Educational Perspective* (Maher, ed, 1987).

Child Protection Training for School Staff

In an ideal world all Heads would ensure that all staff receive training in at least the basic issues of child protection and the procedures to be followed. According to the *Working Together* guide this should be seen as essential for all those involved in the protection of children. A joint approach and joint funding from the DoH and DFE would help to ensure that all schools receive adequate and appropriate training as recommended by the guide.

Schools may receive some help with training from the education welfare service (EWS), the NSPCC or Kidscape. In a number of authorities area social workers have become involved, providing a useful contact for the school staff with those who will be working with them in dealing with future cases. In Rotherham, for example, a number of senior practitioners have set up a liaison system and have provided training in local schools. This initiative was considered so important to the teachers involved that many of them requested further training to be provided in their valuable INSET time (BASPCAN, 1994).

Training materials, which have been tested and found helpful by schools, include Eve Brock's *Child Abuse & the School's Response* from Longman, which gives detailed suggestions for a one-day workshop with handouts on possible signs and symptoms of abuse, the child protection conference, etc, and Michelle Elliott's *Protecting Children* from Kidscape, which is a training pack for front-line carers including teachers.

The Guardian *ad litem* and the School

A person may be appointed to represent the child's interests in court proceedings. This person is called a guardian *ad litem* and will be particularly skilled at communicating with children. As they are required to make an independent assessment of the child's situation, they will usually contact the school to gain information from the Head and teachers. They might wish to spend time in the school to obtain a rounded view of the child's life. Guardians *ad litem* have a right to examine and take copies of any local authority records concerning the child under s.42 of the **Children Act 1989**.

Inspection of a School's Child Protection Procedures

As part of the evaluation of the school in relation to pupils' welfare and guidance (s.7.7 of OFSTED's *Framework for the Inspection of Schools*), inspectors will be looking at the school's child protection policy and procedures, including compliance with the requirements of Circular 4/88, *Working Together for the Protection of Children from Abuse: Procedures Within the Education Service.*

In the technical papers of the OFSTED *Handbook for the Inspection of Schools* there is a paper on child protection (part 5, paper 9) which contains a useful list of effective practice for schools. Schools should:

(a) have an ethos in which children feel secure, their viewpoints are valued, they are encouraged to talk and are listened to

(b) provide suitable support and guidance so that pupils have a range of appropriate adults whom they feel confident to approach if they are in difficulties

(c) work with parents to build an understanding of the school's responsibility to ensure the welfare of all children and a recognition that this may occasionally require cases to be referred to other investigative agencies as a constructive and helpful measure

(d) be vigilant in cases of suspected child abuse, recognising the signs and symptoms, have clear procedures whereby teachers report such cases to the school's senior staff, and are aware of local procedures so that information is effectively passed on to relevant professionals, such as social workers.

Allegations of Abuse by Teachers

Any discussion about child protection in school needs a postscript on the difficulties some schools have experienced with the interpretation of the Children Act when a child alleges abuse by a teacher. During the education conferences of spring 1994, there were anxious and angry complaints about a growing number of allegations, some of which were subsequently proven to be unfounded. The figures had risen from 71 such allegations in 1991 to 158 in 1993, and yet there were only 19 convictions, the majority of allegations resulting in no further action by the police. However, what needs to be remembered here is that although there were only 19 convictions, a large number of cases will not have reached court because of the great difficulty in presenting evidence in such cases.

Unfortunately, some unproven cases caused considerable personal suffering and even damaged the careers of the teachers involved. What is particularly sad about these situations is that they might have been avoided with the help of clear guidelines. According to some, there is nothing wrong with the wording of the legislation, only with the way in which it has been used.

Many schools feel that when the word 'abuse' is spoken by a parent or child, the teacher must be suspended immediately. This is a denial of natural justice and the teacher obviously has the right to know the case against him or her.

Heads should be allowed to carry out initial simple checks, including ensuring that both teacher and pupil were actually in school when the incident was alleged to have happened. There is an urgent need here for clearly thought-out procedures which allow rapid investigation of the grievance in a way which is felt to be just to all parties.

Guidance for schools, *Facing an Allegation of Physical/Sexual Abuse: Guidelines on Practice and Procedures*, has been published by the six unions and the Council of Local Education Authorities (CLEA), which cross-refers to *Working Together* and poses the question each time as to whether suspension — which is allegedly not a sanction — is appropriate. However, there has been some criticism of the guidelines which illustrates the tensions in this very difficult area.

Meanwhile, we need to remind ourselves that the abuse of a principle, in this case the child's right to complain when harmed, does not deny the validity of that principle. Denying children their civil right to complain is clearly not the way forward.

The problem partly is created by having separate government departments with responsibility for children, and even the *Working Together* guide devotes less than a page to education in a document of 117 pages.

CHILDREN LOOKED AFTER BY LOCAL AUTHORITIES

Following the **Children Act 1989**, the term being 'looked after' has now generally replaced the earlier term 'in care'. (The phrase 'in the care of a local authority' is used, however, in the Act in the context of care orders [eg, ss.31 and 34].)

About 55,000 children are looked after in England for a wide variety of reasons, including family breakdown, abuse, neglect or social need. Some children are looked after under voluntary arrangements agreed with the parents who retain parental responsibility. Since April 1991, when the **Children Act 1989** was implemented, there has been an increase in the number of children being looked after through voluntary arrangements, compared to those under a care order.

However, a child considered to be "suffering or likely to suffer significant harm" will be made subject to a care order by the courts, and the social services department then acquires parental responsibility which it shares with the parents. About 70% of children looked after are cared for in a family setting, often with foster carers, and some (about 12%) with family relatives. The remainder are in various types of residential care, mainly children's homes and occasionally in boarding schools.

For children who are being looked after, the school can be a haven from confusion and insecurity, a place where they have the opportunity to be treated as 'ordinary'. When the National Foundation for Educational Research (NFER) carried out a study on such children, one psychologist observed that the particular importance of school for children with problems hinged on the fact that there they could enjoy skills which are tailor-made for the development of self-esteem (Fletcher-Campbell, Hall, 1990). Not surprisingly, children being looked after generally feel low self-regard, and for them the opportunity for personal as well as academic achievement at school may be crucial.

Research over many years has consistently confirmed the impressions of Heads that children in care more frequently have behavioural problems and perform less well than classmates living with their own families. For example, a recent NCB study of young people leaving care found that up to 80% had no formal qualifications, compared with 18% of school-leavers in the general population.

Heads often believe that at least some of the difficulties these children experience in school are due to the low priority which their social workers give to education. The studies confirm this impression but they also point to other causes, such as instability of placement, lack of encouragement, poor study facilities, inadequate support for foster carers and discrimination against children being looked after.

According to the NFER research, 40% of the children had experienced disruption in their schooling, over half had significant problems at school and 24% had been assessed under the **Education Act 1981**. Not surprisingly, they also feature disproportionately among truanting and excluded pupils, and are clearly further disadvantaged by such experiences. In the present competitive climate for places, and improved league tables in schools, such children become even more at risk. For example, the DoH Looking After Children scheme found that in one residential unit *all* the children had been excluded (Jackson, 1993).

The Audit Commission report, *Seen But Not Heard: Co-ordinating Community Child Health and Social Services for Children in Need*, revealed that many children being looked after are not attending schools, with the figure being as high as 40% in one authority (Audit Commission, 1994). The report blamed the lack of co-operation between education, health and social services departments and Phil Youdam of the NCB said the figures showed many children were "falling through the gap" between social services and education.

Circular 13/94 on Children Being Looked After

The key aim of Circular 13/94 on *The Education of Children being looked after by Local Authorities,* in the *Pupils with Problems* series, is to try to change this tendency by promoting effective working partnerships between education and social service agencies to ensure that these children's needs are met and their chances improved (DFE/DoH, 1994).

As well as responding to concern expressed about the educational provision for looked after children during the passage of the **Education Act 1993**, the Circular also fulfils a commitment to respond to the DoH's Utting Report (on children in residential care) and the Warner Report (on the staffing of residential homes). Both these reports highlighted the fact that the education of these children has often been neglected.

The Legal Provisions

Because Circular 13/94 is addressed to social services (being issued under the **Local Authority Social Services Act 1970**), as well as education departments, it will give a legal framework to the partnership which should encourage teachers and social workers to share information and work together for the child — Heads have often complained about how difficult it has been to get information about these children.

When attending case conferences on children who are being looked after, Heads and teachers will find it helpful to know that the care of such children should be subject to rigorous planning (including planning for their education) under the **Arrangements for Placement of Children (General) Regulations 1991** (SI 1991 No. 890) and the **Review of Children's Cases Regulations 1991** (SI 1991 No. 895). The Regulations require the plan to take into consideration the child's educational history, the need to achieve continuity in the child's education and the action to be taken including, if necessary, an assessment under s.167 of the **Education Act 1993**. These care plans must be reviewed at least every six months.

A Project to Give Support for Schools, Children and Families

One way of addressing the needs of such children has been developed in Manchester through a project which provides support for the children, their teachers and carers. This specialist service has been created by closing on-site education units and redeploying 35 teachers to work with all the children whose problems have come to the attention of the social services department. Almost all the children from the units have been maintained successfully in ordinary schools. An evaluation of the project has shown that family and foster breakdown have been greatly reduced.

Action for Schools

Circular 13/94 makes a number of suggestions for schools who have pupils who are being looked after. They include the following.

1. Educational needs should be identified and a plan should set realistic challenges and academic targets. Teachers should always have appropriately high expectations of the child's potential.

2. Children should be involved in decisions taken about them, including those relating to changing school. Under the **Children Act 1989** children must be consulted by the social services department, subject to their age and understanding, about decisions which affect them.

3. As with all parents, schools should encourage foster-parents to support the child's education by discussion and reading at home (research studies have shown a strong compensation correlation between the educational level of the adoptive family and children's achievement).

4. Schools should ensure that full records are passed promptly to a new school.

5. National Curriculum themes, like health education and education for citizenship, careers education, work experience and Records of Achievement (RoA) can provide opportunities for 'looked after' children.

REFERENCES

Audit Commission, *Seen But Not Heard: Co-ordinating Community Child Health and Social Services for Children in Need*. HMSO, 1994.

British Association for the Study and Prevention of Child Abuse and Neglect (BASPCAN), S J Webb, *Child Protection: A Partnership Between Social Services and Education*. BASPCAN 1994 Congress Abstracts, 1994.

Butler-Sloss, E, *Report of the Inquiry into Child Abuse in Cleveland in 1987.* HMSO, 1988.

DES, Circular 4/88: *Working Together for the Protection of Children from Abuse: Procedures within the Education Service*. DES, 1988.

DES, *The Children Act 1989: A Guide for the Education Service*. The Open University, 1991.

DFE/DoH, Circular 13/94: *The Education of Children being looked after by Local Authorities*. DFE, 1994.

Fletcher-Campbell, F, and Hall, C, *Changing Schools? Changing People?* NFER-Nelson, 1990.

Home Office/DoH/DES/Welsh Office, *Working Together Under the Children Act 1989*. HMSO, 1991.

Jackson, S, 'Moving Education up the Social Work Agenda' in *Journal of Education Social Work*, Issue 2, 1993.

Maher, P (ed), *Child Abuse: the Educational Perspective*. Blackwell, 1987.

Masson, J, and Morris, M, *Children Act Manual*. Sweet and Maxwell, 1992.

OFSTED, *Framework for the Inspection of Schools*. HMSO, 1993.

OFSTED, *Handbook for the Inspection of Schools*. HMSO, 1993.

RDHSS, *Report of the Committee on Local Authority and Allied Personal Social Services* (The Seebohm Report). HMSO, 1968.

SOURCES OF ADVICE, INFORMATION AND TRAINING

The following organisations may be useful sources of further information and advice. For addresses and information on the services available from these organisations please see chapter 9.

Childline

The Children's Society

Kidscape

Longman Information and Reference

National Children's Bureau (NCB)

National Society for the Prevention of Cruelty to Children (NSPCC)

The Advisory Council on Alcohol and Drug Education (TACADE)

CHAPTER 4

CHILDREN AS CARERS AND POOR ATTENDERS

CHILDREN WHO CARE FOR PARENTS OR 'PARENT' THE FAMILY

The implementation of the **National Health Service and Community Care Act 1990** has highlighted the difficulties of informal (unpaid) carers in the community (Becker, 1993). Unfortunately most of the discussion on the costs of caring has been about adult carers and has failed to address the issue of child carers or to plan for their future support in the community. There is a dearth of informed literature on child carers, or on the numbers involved, but many schools are aware of a number of pupils who carry a heavy burden looking after a sick or disabled parent and those who 'parent' siblings for a parent who is unable to cope.

This sometimes happens in the context of a single parent family, but it can also develop in a family where there are two parents and the able or well parent may be refusing to provide care for the spouse or siblings, and expecting one child in the family to compensate for their refusal or inability.

We often remain ignorant of the lives that these children may be leading. The very nature of that life may silence them through fear of what may happen if their situation comes to the attention of professionals. They are often anxious about being separated from their families either because they might be taken into care or by the parent being institutionalised. Sometimes their pride or embarrassment about their caring role means that they are reluctant to turn for help to professionals or to talk about their plight to teachers or neighbours.

Adult carers need to be very assertive and confident to shift attention to their own needs, rather than the needs of the one they are caring for. It does not need much imagination to see how much more difficult this must be for children who are carers. Furthermore, the only source of comfort and self-worth available to young carers often comes from the caring process itself, so that in spite of the continual strain and the fact that the traditional parent/child relationship has been turned on its head, they may remain committed to the parent and their task.

The Role of the School

Picking up hints that a child may be in such a situation is a critical role for the school. All the young carers from a Nottingham study (Aldridge and Becker, 1993) felt that what they needed most was someone to talk to and someone who would understand their circumstances, and it is essential for schools to respond sensitively when such children seem to want to talk, are late or absent from school or showing signs of stress.

Not surprisingly, children who look after a parent and who take on a parenting role with siblings, find it hard to accept the child's part they are expected to play at school. Not only will a 'parent' child be suffering from the stress and anxiety of their role but they often resent being treated as a child, and become truculent and confrontational with teachers.

Theoretically, what is required for child carers is exactly what is embodied in the spirit of the new community care legislation, packages of care individually designed to suit the unique needs of each client. In comparison to providing, for example, institutional care for the parent who is being 'looked after' by a child, it would not place a heavy burden on local authority resources to give assistance and relief to young carers. A befriending scheme would be a suitable and inexpensive beginning. Drawing the child's plight to the attention of the local social services department might bring some help and respite, and thus free the pupil to engage in life and work at school.

CHILDREN WHO ARE POOR ATTENDERS

The Education Acts of 1870 and 1880 made school attendance compulsory and empowered LEAs to prosecute parents and remove children from their home when it was considered necessary for their welfare. The Act of 1876 inserted the duty of the parent to cause the child to receive elementary education in the three Rs.

Under the **Education Act 1993**, s.201, the LEA still holds sole responsibility for instituting legal proceedings against parents if they do not register their child at a school or if their child's attendance is irregular or breaks down completely.

Over the last few years, the Government has chosen to put the issue of school attendance at the centre of its education policies. The White Paper, *Choice and Diversity*, listed 'attendance' first in its "imperatives for the 1990s" and funding was created under the Grants for Education Support and Training (GEST) programme to support schemes to help schools and the wider community to combat truancy.

Truancy-watch Projects

A number of truancy-watch projects have been set up with the aim of involving the community, police and schools in combating non-attendance. Although truancy-watch projects may have a part in a strategy to improve attendance, the Home Office says that in fact neither police officers nor education welfare officers (EWOs) have any *legal* authority to stop children who are not committing an offence.

Concern has been expressed that truancy patrols tend to be superficial exercises, tackling the symptom rather than the underlying malady. When young people are discouraged away from, for example, shopping centres they may find themselves in more dangerous environments, such as empty houses, or mixing with people who may be only too keen to take advantage of their vulnerability. Paradoxically, therefore, truancy patrols may actually increase the chances of young people being at risk of exploitation or other harm. It is also thought by some that merely forcing children back into school will not solve the problem.

Schools are well aware that the reasons why children do not attend school are complex and varied. For any particular child they may include a mixture of social, psychological and institutional reasons. For many in a generation with poor expectations of the future, there may be some correlation with their lack of faith in the benefits of education. It is no longer a simple matter of persuading a young person that they should go to school because this will ensure that they will have a job when they leave.

To make things more difficult, just as the Government is calling for something to be done about truancy, the service most helpful to schools with attendance problems, the education welfare service (EWS), is facing cuts in staffing levels. The service is to be a mandatory exception from delegation, but the reduced and reducing budgets of LEAs make it vulnerable to cuts — at present there are only about 2800 EWOs for a school population of nearly nine million. This is despite much research showing that preventive programmes which support services like the EWS can provide are, with nursery education, the most positive indicators for reducing the number of pupils likely to drift into truancy or offending.

Guidance on Categorisation of Absence

Heads will find the new DFE guidance on *School Attendance, Policy and Practice on Categorisation of Absence* (DFE, 1994) helpful in clarifying areas of uncertainty created by the division of absences into authorised and unauthorised under the **Education (Pupils' Attendance Records) Regu-**

lations 1991 (SI 1991 No. 1582). The paper reminds Heads that only the school, within the context of the law, can approve absence, and gives advice on making decisions in a range of tricky situations including the following.

1. Minding the house/looking after brothers or sisters

This is an area in which the Head has discretion whether or not to grant leave of absence, but the Secretary of State would expect this to be done only in exceptional circumstances. Examples may include where a single parent has fallen seriously ill and there are no relatives nearby who can help to look after younger children. The parent may then have little choice but to look to an older child to help out until alternative arrangements can be made. In such circumstances the absence may be authorised while urgent contact is made with the education welfare service (EWS), which may in turn wish to involve social services. The school should take appropriate steps to provide school work for the pupil, and set a time limit and review date.

2. Family bereavement

This can be a particularly traumatic event in any young person's life. Schools should respond sensitively and have discretion to authorise leave of absence to attend funerals or associated events, but if the pupil is absent for more than the agreed period, early contact should be made with the family and the EWS.

3. Family holidays and extended trips overseas during term time

Under regulation 12 of the **Education (Schools and Further Education) Regulations 1981** (SI 1981 No. 1086), the Head has a discretionary power to grant leave for a holiday, but only in exceptional circumstances may this exceed more than two weeks in any year. Factors which may be relevant to the Head's decision include:

(a) the nature and purpose of the trip

(b) the duration and impact on the child's education

(c) circumstances of family and wishes of parents

(d) the distance being travelled and the expense

(e) the overall attendance pattern of the child.

If the parents do not gain permission before the holiday/visit overseas, or if the child is away in excess of the period agreed, then the time should be treated as unauthorised absence. Such behaviour would not normally be sufficient cause for a child to be struck off the roll.

Where the school is experiencing difficulties in determining whether absences should be authorised, the education welfare officer (EWO) should be consulted. The guidance reminds schools that the EWS constitutes a valuable resource for schools, both in its own right and as a channel to other agencies.

Strategies for Schools

The question which needs to be addressed is — what can the school do to motivate pupils to want to come to school in spite of the many pressures and temptations to stay away? The following list describes a few strategies for dealing with absenteeism which some schools have found helpful.

1. Involve all teachers, the EWO, parents and pupils in establishing a written whole school attendance policy.
2. Identify a manager who will take on, with enthusiasm, the role of overall responsibility for attendance matters.
3. Make it clear to new parents that the school cares about each child's attendance by a clear policy statement in the prospectus, and through swift follow-up on non-attendance.
4. Agree that good school attendance should be the concern of all teachers and not just a chore for pastoral staff or heads of year.
5. Establish regular meetings to identify, assist and monitor children who do not attend regularly. (This can provide a useful support group for the school, bringing in the EWO, school nurse or medical officer, educational psychologist and social worker as required.)

6.   Design a home-school agreement which includes a statement that parents will do all they can to ensure their child's regular attendance and discourage lateness.

7.   Send letters (personal rather than standard formats) to parents commending good and improved attendance.

8.   Ensure that, when pupils return to school after an absence, they receive positive responses and help with work missed.

9.   With younger children, identify those 'at risk' before they transfer to secondary schools, and plan ways to support them.

10. Use governors, eg a sub-committee to meet poor attenders, discussing their difficulties and encouraging them to report back on any improvements.

11. Design contracts with non-attenders which state clearly what can be expected of the pupil and the school. The EWO can help with such a programme.

12. Set attainment goals for individuals or class or year groups, and/or hold competitions for the best or most markedly improved attendance.

13. Discuss with truants any difficulties or dislikes they may have about particular lessons. Attendance research commissioned by the DFE found that the most common reason given by truants for truanting was the wish to avoid particular lessons. (DFE, 1993.)

14. Use systems for checking which will help to eliminate 'internal truancy'.

Co-operation is the crucial emphasis of these strategies, taking into account all the possible influences on the child's reluctance or inability to attend school. Such an approach is also in line with the requirements of the **Children Act 1989** when making a request to the court for an education supervision order: the court must be given information about what has been done already by the school to try to resolve the problem and what action is planned for the pupil, parent, EWO and the school if the court grants an order.

OFSTED Handbook for the Inspection of Schools

The Handbook states that for classes and years where levels of attendance fall below 90%, inspectors should investigate the causes and the school's actions to improve attendance (OFSTED, 1993). Evidence about school attendance should include:

(a) the school's policy

(b) any other documentation on attendance, eg 'compact' schemes, reward systems, information to parents and pupils on expectations, follow-up of absences

(c) pupils' records, including correspondence with home and the EWS

(d) discussion with pupils, parents and staff, and

(e) pupils' punctuality in arriving at school and in class.

YOUNG CHILDREN WHO ARE LEFT AT HOME ALONE

Sometimes a Head becomes aware that a child is being left alone at home, and queries the legal position of parents of 'latch-key kids' and what they can usefully say in advising such parents. In this situation, the law is actually not very helpful: it does not specify an age at which children can be left alone nor say at what age young people can babysit.

Schools, however, will find a recently published leaflet for parents from the National Society for the Prevention of Cruelty to Children (NSPCC) helpful to give to parents. The leaflet gives clear advice, for example, that:

(a) babies or young children should never be left at home alone (whether sleeping or awake), not even for a few minutes

(b) most children under about 13 are not mature enough to cope with an emergency and should not be left alone for more than a very short time

(c) no child or young person under at least 16 should be left alone at night, and

(d) children under 16 cannot be held responsible for any harm that happens to a child in their care.

The leaflet, *Home Alone*, is available free, with an SAE, from the NSPCC (see chapter 9 for address).

YOUNG PEOPLE WHO RUN AWAY FROM HOME

Despite the fact that the **Children Act 1989** provided a legal framework for setting up refuges for young people, there are still very few projects in the country working specifically with young people who run away.

The Glaxo Refuge based in north London, a safe house providing accommodation for up to two weeks for young runaways under 16, is one of the first to be certificated under the Act, and provides a key worker to give advice. It also arranges some social skills, arts and other education sessions, as well as providing pocket money and facilities to meet their families on neutral ground.

The Children's Society runs a few similar projects in various parts of the country including a 'Safe House' in Leeds (addresses of such projects from the Children's Society). A recent report from the Society revealed that there is a good deal of running away from home, and that, although in the past it was thought to happen mainly with children in care, it is primarily a 'family problem' with the most common reason being an abusive home situation and affects young people from all backgrounds and settings. Young people usually run from a distressing situation rather than setting out in a spirit of adventure (The Children's Society, 1993).

REFERENCES

Aldridge, J and Becker, S, 'Punishing Children for Caring: The Hidden Costs of Young Carers' in *Children & Society*, Vol 7, No 4, 1993.

Becker, S, 'Personal Social Services' in Catterall, P, (ed), *Contemporary Britain: An Annual Review 1993*. Blackwell, 1993.

The Children's Society, *Hidden Truths*. The Children's Society, 1993.

DFE, *Truancy in English Secondary Schools*. HMSO, 1993.

DFE, *School Attendance: Policy and Practice on Categorisation of Absence*. DFE, 1994.

OFSTED, *Handbook for the Inspection of Schools*. HMSO, 1993.

SOURCES OF ADVICE, INFORMATION AND TRAINING

The following organisations may be useful sources of further information and advice. For addresses and information on the services available from these organisations please see chapter 9.

The Children's Society

National Society for the Prevention of Cruelty to Children (NSPCC)

Training Advisory Group (TAG)

CHAPTER 5

DRUG AND SOLVENT ABUSE

DRUGS AND DRUG EDUCATION IN SCHOOLS

One in three young people have tried illegal drugs by the age of 20 and, according to a recent national audit on drug misuse, chemicals such as LSD and Ecstasy are now firmly established in the youth culture (ISDD, 1993). The study revealed that use of some hallucinogenic drugs and stimulants has doubled since the early 1980s: in 1983 less than 1–2% of school-leavers said they had tried LSD, and Ecstasy was unknown. About 10% (more than half a million young people) have tried amphetamines. In some areas the percentage of schoolchildren actually experimenting with drugs may be very high indeed — one London borough project claims it is about 70% locally.

Manchester University researchers, following a representative sample of young people from north west England, believe that their figures of 71% in "drug-offer" situations and 47% in "ever tried" an illicit drug, in their GCSE year, is a reliable indicator of the 'normalisation' of drugs among this generation. The latest YMCA research found that 50% of young people are offered drugs at school.

These findings suggest that not only has the illegal drugs market blended into the 'legal' world of school, party, pub and club, but that this market is now offering a wide variety of products sometimes as cheaply as the price of a couple of bottles of strong lager. LSD, for instance, is now sold in neat, attractive acid blotters for about £3 (*The Guardian*, 21.2.94). Ecstasy, whose medical name is MDMA, first crossed the Atlantic in the early 1980s, and became a common part of the rave scene. Some deaths have been attributed to taking Ecstasy tablets, which in certain users may cause massive internal damage and heart attack.

In parts of the country a major epidemic of drug abuse has spread via the clubs into schools and youth centres. It is difficult to ascertain how led by fashion most young abusers are, but if they see their peers taking drugs and consider it trendy, weaker individuals will often follow suit.

There is some encouraging news for schools, however, which comes from an Exeter University survey for the Schools Health Education Unit. It found that although a third of 15- and 16-year-olds had been offered or encouraged to try cannabis, the number actually experimenting with drugs was much lower, suggesting that many teenagers do resist pressure to use drugs (Balding, 1994). It is clear, therefore, that drug education, which shows young people how to resist such offers and make responsible choices for themselves, is essential to any programme aiming to reduce drug use among young people.

The DFE Grants for Education Support and Training (GEST) funding for health education co-ordinators (HECs) came to an end in April 1993, and although most authorities thought their work was valuable, particularly in supporting and helping with training on drugs in schools, the posts have been cut in many authorities.

Drug Education

A few months after the ending of this DFE funding, the Home Office Advisory Council on the Misuse of Drugs (ACMD) published a report on *Drug Education in Schools: the Need for a New Impetus* (ACMD, 1993) calling for:

(a) high quality classroom drug education on a national scale

(b) consistent national standards for teacher training, and

(c) a trained co-ordinator in each school to take the lead role on drug education.

Drug education can be addressed in a number of subjects such as science, history, geography, PE, RE and drama, but it is important that a diversity of approach does not lead to conflicting or inconsistent messages. The school's drug education programme needs to be carefully co-ordinated and planned within the overall context of health education which emphasises the benefits of a healthy lifestyle and enables young people to make informed and responsible choices.

The DFE booklet, *Drug Misuse and the Young*, advises that this sort of approach is likely to be more effective — particularly in the longer term — than those which seek to shock or frighten, or which target particular drugs. A 'shock-horror' strategy is more likely to entertain young people rather than put them off (DFE, 1992). It is unfortunate that much of the material designed to put them off taking drugs seems rather to offer them the risks and excitement for which some young people yearn. A London unit for 'disruptive' pupils found that the most effective drug education emphasised the profit a few exploiters gained by getting young people hooked on expensive substances (Lovey, 1992).

Many adolescents can become quite usefully indignant when they are reminded that drug-related habits are expensive and that they are being conned by dealers and by the advertisements of the tobacco and alcohol industries. These young people are more sophisticated than we sometimes allow: they are often keenly interested in the relationship between themselves and the material world, and the means by which that world is produced, presented and 'sold' to them.

Undoubtedly one of the worst aspects of drug abuse is that it may drive those who become dependent on it into crime in order to pay for the addiction. The Glasgow police force, for example, has found that at least 50% of crime in Glasgow is drug-related. According to youth workers in Moss Side, Manchester, the financial incentive to becoming a drug-dealer is massive. The slippery slope into drug-pushing can begin when children (many of them under 15) are recruited by dealers to act as look-outs for police, then they may become "runners" delivering drugs and finally dealers in their own right.

National Curriculum Requirements

Drug education is part of the statutory order for National Curriculum science. Activities should allow children at:

(a) *key stage 1* — to understand the role of drugs as medicines

(b) *key stage 2* — to be introduced to the fact that while all medicines are drugs, not all drugs are medicines: be aware of the effects of drug abuse

(c) *key stage 3* — to study ways in which the healthy functioning of the human body may be promoted or disrupted by the use and misuse of medicines and drugs, and

(d) *key stage 4* — to study the effects of solvents, alcohol, tobacco and other drugs on the way the human body functions.

As drug education is also a key area of study in the cross-curricular theme of health education, *Curriculum Guidance Vol 5* gives detailed guidance on what drug issues should be covered at each stage and how these might be integrated into the wider curriculum (NCC, 1990).

How Young Should Drug Education Begin?

Some very young children are exposed to drug use by those they live with and most children develop a quite sophisticated perception of drugs through television at an early age. The 10- to 14-year-old period is the crucial age at which experimentation commonly begins and education needs to start two to three years before the likely age of experimentation, according to the Home Office report. Some youth workers claim that by the time youngsters get to secondary school, it is too late. This is not only true for well publicised inner-city areas with drug problems like Moss Side: 23 under-16s, for example, were recently arrested in Scarborough for possession of LSD, some of them as young as 12. The drug dealers are getting younger all the time and so are their targets.

The School's Relationship with Parents

Heads may be worried that designing a policy for the school and discussing it with parents might lead them to think that the school has a 'drugs problem'. Not having a policy, however, may result in problems being discovered at a dangerously late stage.

In fact, an open and positive school policy, stressing the school's pastoral role and its proactive approach to drug and health education, can be reassuring for parents. Involving parents helps to ensure that they will reinforce the school's work. Parents and pupils also need to know that the school will inform parents if they discover that a child is a drug user.

For parents as well as teachers, the most helpful advice, when confronted with suspected or confirmed drug use, is to think before acting — don't panic. Over-reaction all too often makes things worse (Pollard, 1993). Approaching the situation with anger, anxiety or, in the case of parents, guilt is only likely to make the child or adolescent defensive and resistant to discussion or treatment.

Secondary Heads might like to order copies of a usefully down-to-earth leaflet for parents, *Adolescents and Drugs*, published by Exploring Parenthood, which also has an advice line (see chapter 9).

Managing Drug-related Incidents

The school policy on how to deal with pupils found possessing, selling or using drugs (including volatile substances, tobacco and alcohol) on school property needs to be clear and well publicised. Such a policy helps to avoid making panic decisions and ensures consistent responses whenever an incident occurs. It should deal both with ways to help the pupil with a drug misuse problem and with the disciplinary measures to be taken. Heads may find it helpful to contact their police liaison officer for advice when formulating a policy.

According to DFE Circular 10/94, *Exclusions from School*, the Secretary of State considers that it would be neither possible nor desirable to prescribe centrally every incident where exclusion would be an appropriate response. However, schools may decide that exclusion would be justified when a pupil commits a serious criminal offence, such as drug trafficking. In such a case it is important to remember that exclusion without simultaneous recourse to medical support may further endanger the pupil's welfare.

Legal Requirements in Relation to Drugs

It is useful for Heads to know that all LEAs should have formulated guidelines on the steps to take and contacts to make in dealing with drug-related incidents. An HMI report on GEST funding found that schools were often not aware of these.

Schools cannot ignore the influence that some older pupils involved in drugs have on some of the more vulnerable younger pupils. Clearly, lawbreaking cannot be condoned on school premises, and those who are profiting from the sale of prohibited substances must be dealt with by the community, not the school.

Under s.8 of the **Misuse of Drugs Act 1971** it is an offence to knowingly permit the production or supply of any controlled drug on the premises or the preparation or smoking of cannabis or opium on the premises. If a Head confiscates drugs from a pupil, or finds drugs, they should be destroyed or handed to someone authorised to possess illegal drugs, usually a police officer. The Act allows an individual to take possession of an illegal drug in order to prevent someone else committing an offence.

Training, Recognising the Signs and Responding to Questions

Although early detection of substance misuse may be a key part of prevention, any list of possible signs holds the danger of jumping to false conclusions, not least because all adolescents go through such a confusing range of physical, hormonal, emotional and behavioural changes. The

DFE booklet, *Drug Misuse and the Young* (DFE/Welsh Office, 1992), contains a list of warnings which includes changes in attendance habits, unusual outbreaks of temper, marked swings of mood, restlessness or irritability — much of which sounds like a fair description of most adolescent behaviour. However, other symptoms may be more accurate indicators, eg sores or rashes on the mouth or nose, loss of weight, ashen skin colour, heavy use of scents to disguise smell of drugs, sunglasses to hide dilated or constricted pupils, lack of appetite, nausea or vomiting.

Teachers should all have a basic awareness training so they will have some understanding of signs, symptoms and effects of drug use. This will enable them to discuss drug use with their pupils in a rational and non-judgmental way and give accurate information on the risks of drug use. Just becoming informed about the main drugs used by young people can give teachers confidence when pupils ask questions.

The Institute for the Study of Drug Dependence (ISDD) has published a book, *Drug Issues for Schools*, which has a detailed section on designing an effective whole school policy and useful background information for teachers on the legal aspects, first aid and the main drugs (Chapman, 1992).

A school might usefully decide to provide joint training sessions for teachers, parents and governors. One school involved the pupils and the whole school staff, including the school nurse, in a health week for which the pupils designed posters, leaflets, collected information, etc. Participation in such training could usefully be extended to the Youth Service, local health visitors, GPs, the District Health Authority health education officer, and the Local Drug Prevention Team in areas where there is one.

SOLVENT MISUSE

Solvent misuse is the inhalation of the fumes from a number of household products in order to get intoxicated. The substances used include solvent-based adhesives (glue-sniffing), butane gas (cigarette lighter refills), aerosols, thinners and correcting fluid. When the chemicals are breathed in deeply through the mouth or nose they cause a rapid intoxication within 15–30 seconds, which can last for up to 30 minutes. As not all the substances are solvents, it is also known as volatile substance abuse.

Solvent misuse is not illegal, but the **Intoxicating Substances Supply Act 1985** makes it an offence to supply, to a person under 18, a substance which the supplier knows, or believes, will be used to achieve intoxication. The easy availability of the products is clearly a factor in the widespread nature of the problem.

Since it is not illegal, it is difficult to record in a systematic way and to judge its extent. One study suggests that up to 10% of school age children have experimented with volatile substances (Chadwick, 1991). Both boys and girls experiment with solvents, but girls seem to do so in less dangerous ways: the mortality figures are much higher for males. Although rates seem to be highest in regions with the most social deprivation, solvent misuse is present in all social classes.

Sniffing is often concentrated for an epidemic period on a particular estate, in a school or a residential home. In the experimental or recreational stages it is often a group activity but dependent users are more likely to sniff on their own. Only a small percentage go on to become long-term users and such dependency is often a symptom of the young person's attempt to escape from unbearable problems at home or other severe emotional or social difficulties.

Effects of Solvent Misuse

Inhaling solvents results in rapid intoxication and euphoria. It can also cause depression, hallucinations, delusions, slurring of speech, lack of co-ordination, sudden mood swings, nausea and coughing bouts. Chadwick's study found that, although sniffers performed less well, when other factors were taken into account, in tests of vocabulary and verbal intelligence, the misuse of solvents by secondary school pupils was unlikely to result in neuro-psychological damage. A large number of children may 'sniff' for a while without any physical or psychological scars.

Solvent misuse is, however, intrinsically very dangerous. The number of children's deaths from solvent misuse is alarming: 500 over the last four years from suffocation, through cardiac arrest, inhalation of vomit or serious accidents while 'high'.

Symptoms of Solvent Misuse

Some of the clues which schools might watch for include:

(a) chemical smells on breath or clothing

(b) rapid mood swings from anger to giggling and euphoria

(c) loss of concentration, truancy and a drop in school performance

(d) spots around mouth or nose, constant headaches, sore throats or runny nose, and

(e) finding aerosols, lighter fuel refills or plastic bags (often crisp bags) with glue in them.

Discussion with Parents

Because the use of solvents is a fairly recent phenomenon, most parents are unlikely to have encountered 'sniffing' while they were teenagers, and unfamiliarity heightens the anxiety they feel if they suspect that their children may be involved. Parents also worry that once immersed in any drug subculture teenagers are vulnerable to other addictions such as alcohol and hard drugs. A leaflet for parents, *Children and Solvents*, from Exploring Parenthood will be helpful for those who are concerned (see chapter 9 for address).

The leaflet advises parents that they are not powerless but are the most important influence upon their child's behaviour, although it may not feel like that. It suggests talking about what is happening at school in order to find out about any pressures or anxieties the teenager is facing and advises the parent to talk to the school as it is unlikely the child is a solitary user. Perhaps the child has got involved with a group of tougher pupils, who are sniffing, as a way of coping with bullying and thus showing that he or she too can be 'bad'.

Education and Solvent Misuse

As with drug education, there has been a move away from shock-horror techniques and towards an emphasis on the skills which young people need to use to negotiate their way safely in a drug-using culture. Re-Solv, an organisation which was formed by manufacturers in order to ensure safer use of their products, receives funding from the Department of Health, and offers information and training (see chapter 9).

REFERENCES

ACMD, *Drug Education in Schools: The Need for a New Impetus.* HMSO, 1993.

Balding, J, *Young People in 1993.* Exeter University, 1994.

Chapman, C, *Drugs Issues for Schools.* Institute for the Study of Drug Dependence (ISDD), 1992.

Chadwick, O, et al, *Solvent Abuse: Population-based Neuro-psychological Study.* Springer-Verlag, 1991.

DFE, *Drug Misuse and the Young.* DFE/Welsh Office, 1992.

DFE, Circular 10/94: *Exclusions from School.* DFE, 1994.

ISDD, *National Audit of Drug Misuse in Britain 1992.* Institute for the Study of Drug Dependence, 1993.

Lovey, J, *Teaching Troubled and Troublesome Adolescents.* David Fulton, 1992.

NCC, *Curriculum Guidance 5, Health Education.* National Curriculum Council, 1990.

Pollard, D, 'The School Student and Drug Use' in Alsop, P and McCaffrey, T (eds), *How to Cope with Childhood Stress.* Longman, 1993.

SOURCES OF ADVICE, INFORMATION AND TRAINING

The following organisations may be useful sources of further information and advice. For addresses and information on the services available from these organisations please see chapter 9.

Healthwise Ltd

Institute for the Study of Drug Dependence

Lifeline

National Children's Bureau (NCB)

Release

Re-solve

The Advisory Council on Alcohol and Drug Education (TACADE)

CHAPTER 6

CHILDREN IN NEED AND CHILDREN WITH SEN

CHILDREN IN NEED AND SPECIAL EDUCATIONAL NEEDS

A distinction is drawn in Part III of the **Children Act 1989** between children in need and other children. A child is defined, in s.17(10), as a child in need if:

(a) he or she is unlikely to achieve or maintain a reasonable standard of health or development without the provision for him or her of services by the local authority

(b) his or her health or development is likely to be significantly impaired without the provision for him or her of such services

(c) he or she is disabled.

Children in School Who are Children in Need

Clearly many, if not virtually all, the children discussed in this book would come under these definitions. What must be asked is how does the legislation affect work in school with such children? The most important thing for Heads to know is that under this legislation children in need and their families have rights to services. If the school is concerned about the level of support such families are being offered, Heads may wish to discuss this with the local social services department. If you are wondering if a pupil might be defined as a 'child in need' by social services, it is helpful to know when you turn to the Children Act's definition quoted above that the Act defines 'health' as physical or mental health and 'development' as physical, intellectual, emotional, social or behavioural development, (s.17 [11]).

Ruth Sinclair, Director of Research at the National Children's Bureau, believes that by the legal definition anyone who is not receiving appropriate educational provision could be called a 'child in need' (Sinclair, 1994). Some authorities have decided to include children who are not attending a school and children who have been excluded from school in their local authority definition of children in need.

Children in Need and Preventive Services

The **Children Act 1989** is based on the concept that children are generally best looked after within their own families (immediate or extended) as long as this is consistent with the child's welfare. The Act advises that local authorities should try to support and work with families without resort to legal proceedings. They must protect children who are suffering from significant harm caused by abuse or family breakdown, but otherwise unwarranted intervention in family life should be avoided.

The duty (note 'duty', not 'power') to provide a range of support services for children in need is, therefore, seen as a preventive measure to help families carry out their responsibilities in bringing up their children, and to avoid family breakdown or the sort of crisis which might necessitate the child being put under the care of the authority. When planning and providing such services, the local authority must take into account the views of children and parents, and also be aware of the particular perspectives and needs of different races, cultures, religions and languages.

There are new and very wide statutory duties placed upon the local authority. It is true that the preventive framework of this section of the **Children Act 1989** demands a level of provision which is practically impossible for most local government departments to meet. Some people have been concerned about how the Act's fine but demanding aspirations can be met without extra resources. The basic problem is that both LEAs and local social services authorities (LSSAs) (the same councils, in exercise of different statutory functions) face both problems: newly defined responsibilities and no additional resources.

Just as education departments have been caught up in SEN assessments and statementing rather than meeting the whole spectrum of special educational needs, so social services departments have tended to a narrow definition of 'in need'. As might be expected, a national study on the implementation of s.17 found that many local authorities are defining 'in need' narrowly to cover children at risk of significant harm, rather than placing emphasis on offering support services before problems become too serious. The Audit Commission report, *Seen But Not Heard* (1994), claimed that many authorities were not identifying children in need as required by the Act and only a quarter visited by the Commission had developed a joint strategic plan.

The important point here, however, is that it is right that the needs of these children and their families should be drawn to the attention of social services by schools, and that it is in the children's interests that we should use legislation — in this case the Children Act — to argue on their behalf. It is also important to remember that LEAs and LSSAs are the same councils and that s.19 requires LEA involvement in the triennial reviews of services for the under-eights.

Heads may find a booklet from the University of Leicester — clearly written and inexpensive at £3 — a helpful guide to Part III of the Act which is about children in need (Shaw, et al, 1990).

Information on Services for Children in Need

Knowing in detail what services are recommended by the Children Act for families will help Heads in their negotiations with social workers.

Firstly, s.19 and Schedule 2 to the Act require local authorities to review and publish information about all the services (day care and educational) that are provided for children under eight years of age (eg out-of-school clubs, holiday schemes, adventure playgrounds, extended day playgroups). A good starting point might, therefore, be to ask the local social services department for this published information, so you will have it available when talking to a family who might benefit from such help.

Secondly, children who are in need, according to the Act, should be provided with appropriate after-school care and care in school holidays.

Thirdly, Schedule 2, paragraph 8 states that every local authority shall make such provision as it considers appropriate for the following services to be available for the families of children in need:

(a) advice, guidance and counselling

(b) occupational, social, cultural or recreational activities

(c) home help (which may include laundry facilities)

(d) facilities for, or assistance with, travelling to and from home for the purpose of taking advantage of any other service provided under this Act or of any similar service

(e) assistance to enable the child concerned and his or her family to have a holiday.

Fourthly, for any child within the local authority's area who has SEN, the Act requires social services to assist LEAs with the provision of services, s.27(4). (Although s.27 [4] has been repealed by the **Education Act 1993**, paragraph 147 of schedule 19 from 1.9.94, the law on co-operation has been strengthened by s.166 of the 1993 Act [see page 78].)

The Legal Requirement to Provide Family Centres

According to the guidance to the Children Act, Vol 2 (*Family Support, Day Care and Educational Provision for Young Children* [DoH, 1991]) there was little statistical information (at least before the Act's requirement to publish such information), about how school age children use their leisure time, or the services available to look after them while parents are at work, following higher education or otherwise not available outside the school day and in the holidays. It is thought that among children of primary school age about 20% return to an empty house — the so-called 'latchkey children'.

The Children Act brought the concept of 'family centres' into legislation for the first time. Under the general duty to promote the upbringing of children by their families (s.17), the authority has a duty to provide family centres (again, as it considers appropriate for children in its area). Family centres cover provision for:

(a) occupational, social, cultural or recreational activities

(b) advice, guidance or counselling, or

(c) accommodation while receiving advice, guidance or counselling.

A survey in 1989 noted 352 such centres in England and Wales, of which 57% were run by statutory bodies and the rest by voluntary agencies. A growing number of these centres have been concentrating on clients referred for child abuse or neglect, providing intensive treatment for a small number of children and, usually, mothers. Although such centres do important work in helping mothers with management skills, parents often feel stigmatised by their restricted enrolment and even that they are being forced to attend under threat of losing their children.

Centres with a more open community and neighbourhood enrolment and an ethos which can be preventive rather than treatment orientated would be more in line with the concepts of the Children Act — it would be a pity if they were to lose out in the struggles for funding. Perhaps in future, some Heads might think about using the school for such a family centre. Any Heads interested in such an idea might care to look at Bob Holman's book, *A New Deal for Social Welfare*. Although it does not suggest the use of a school for a venue, it does give a good description and analysis of the work of community family centres and concludes that they draw in a variety of users, but do not exclude individuals with severe personal problems. On the contrary, Holman feels that all parents can more easily walk into a centre which is not marked out as a place for those with particular difficulties (Holman, 1993).

Following the Children Act's principle that departments must work together (which is discussed in the next section), a jointly funded parents' room in a school could perhaps be developed as such a centre.

Co-operation and Consultation between Education and Social Services

Although responsibility for implementation rests mainly with the social services (according to the Act's Guidance (Vol.2) on *Family Support, Day Care and Educational Provision*) the Act is directed at the local authority *as a whole* and cannot succeed without collaboration at all levels.

Under ss.27 and 47 of the Act, LEAs have a duty to assist local authorities in the exercise of their statutory responsibilities for children in need or for child protection. In a similar manner, the **Education Act 1993** acknowledges that the LEA may call upon the District Health Authority (DHA) or local authority (ie social services) for assistance with any of the LEA functions under Part III which is about children with SEN. Working together, therefore, is a requirement of law for teachers and social workers and can no longer be left to chance or good practice.

In the past, part of the difficulty in working together has been the defensive insistence of both professions on separate and clearly defined roles — exemplified by the familiar cry: "I'm a teacher not a social worker" (Webb, 1991).

However, three years down the road, common languages are being found, and there is more acceptance that we must break down barriers between the professions so that we can address the needs of the whole child, and make corporate and cost effective plans for future provision.

There are a number of situations, therefore, where Heads should be prepared to co-operate with social services, including:

- identifying the number of children in need in the locality

- assessing individual children who may be in need
- establishing the register of children with disabilities, and
- making an audit of existing provision.

The DES publication *The Children Act 1989: A Guide for the Education Service* states that identifying the provision locally will help to pinpoint gaps that need to be filled, and where there is duplication (DES, 1991). Most schools will feel that the problems are about gaps rather than duplication.

As assessments may be carried out at the same time under the Children Act, the **Education Act 1981** and the **Disabled Persons Act 1986**, it can readily be seen that it is both logical and necessary for teachers and social workers to work together.

CHILDREN WITH DISABILITIES

One of the tasks on which the departments of the authority need to collaborate is in establishing a register of children with disabilities — in fact, this is what might be called a "must do" duty. The Act defines disability with the rather archaic **National Assistance Act 1948** definition:

blind, deaf or dumb, or suffers from mental disorder of any kind or is substantially and permanently handicapped by illness, injury or congenital deformity or such other ability as may be prescribed

It was considered necessary to use this definition to ensure that these children will continue to qualify for services after the age of 18.

In spite of the definition, the Act is a good step forward for the 360,000 children under 16 with one or more disabilities (figure from the Office of Population Census Surveys, OPCS). It brings these children into mainstream legislation for the first time, and it requires authorities to design provision for them which will minimise the effects of their disabilities and so allow them to lead lives which are as normal as possible (Schedule 2). Children with disabilities are treated by the Act first as children, and then as persons with a disability. They therefore benefit from safeguards which were unavailable to them under previous legislation unless they were in the care of the authority.

It is important to reassure parents that the register is definitely not in any sense an 'at risk' or 'child protection' register. Inclusion on the register is voluntary; parents will see what is written and the purpose of the information will be to help social services, education and health departments plan better services.

Involving Children with Disabilities in Planning for Their Future

The **Children Act 1989** places new duties on social services departments to involve the children themselves when planning their futures. Learning to make well-informed choices — and making and surviving mistakes — should be part of every child's experience. Children and young people should be given the chance to exercise choice, and their views should be taken seriously if they are unhappy about the arrangements made for them.

Heads and teachers, with their skills in communicating with children with special needs and disabilities, can be invaluable in the process of assessment and planning. Should the child have complex needs or communication difficulties, arrangements must be made to establish his or her views, according to the Children Act guidance. It is felt that even children with severe learning disabilities or very limited expressive language can communicate preferences if asked in the right way by those who understand their needs and have the relevant skills to listen. Assumptions should not be made about 'categories' of children with disabilities who cannot share in decision-making or give consent to or refuse examination, assessment or treatment (DoH, 1991A).

Respite care, day care and holiday provision recommended by the legislation can all help these children and ease the load for their hard-pressed families, making it more likely that they will be able to remain with their families. When a child with SEN is being assessed, the guidance states that social services could support parents, particularly where the family has a range of needs unrelated to the educational assessment. For example, counselling and other supportive services might be provided for parents whose children have behavioural difficulties, physical disabilities or learning difficulties.

Again, although resources may be scarce, Heads and others in contact with such families, who have information about the Children Act, can help them to argue for the services to which the Act gives them an entitlement. According to Philippa Russell, the Director for the Council for Disabled Children, the Act offers important new possibilities for children with disabilities and their families, but its success will depend upon parents and professionals not only encouraging their local authorities to develop better services but also helping to evaluate and monitor those services which do exist (Russell, 1992).

An explanatory leaflet on the Act, *The Children Act: A Guide for Parents*, says that the Act is about how society believes children should be cared for. It creates law about the upbringing of children to ensure that the best is achieved for this and future generations. Its aim is to help children in need get the best deal possible by providing services to their families (DoH, 1991B).

Distinguishing Between SEN and Children in Need

Understandably, schools may sometimes feel uncertain about what distinction should be drawn between children in need and children with SEN. As has been suggested in this section, many of the pupils with SEN, as defined under the **Education Act 1993**, will also be assessed as 'in need' under the **Children Act 1989**.

However, the DES guide to the Children Act says that we should keep a clear distinction between these two definitions and recognise that they are serving different purposes and have different implications (DES, 1991). Whereas SEN is linked to educational needs specifically, 'in need' is intended to lead to the broader range of support services, described above, to enable families facing troubles of different kinds to look after their children themselves.

81

Although the distinction may be made in the name of bureaucratic tidiness, professionals working with children know that the reality is often more complex than that. DES Circular 22/89, for example, admitted that the extent to which a learning difficulty hinders a child's development does not depend solely on the nature and severity of that difficulty. The personal resources and attributes of the child, as well as the level of help and support provided at home, will also be significant factors.

THE EDUCATION ACT 1993 AND THE CODE OF PRACTICE

For those children who have SEN and are also 'in need' under the Children Act — and as such are part of the pupil population which this book addresses — the **Education Act 1993** has created some welcome changes.

Part III of the 1993 Act re-enacts virtually the whole of the **Education Act 1981** and includes some changes which were proposed in the White Paper, *Choice and Diversity* (DFE, 1992), and the DFE consultation document, *Special Educational Needs: Access to the System*, including:

(a) giving parents the right to express a preference for a particular ordinary or special maintained school for their child

(b) a requirement for any school named in a statement, including a GM school, to admit the child after consultation and provided that certain conditions are met, eg efficient education for other pupils, efficient use of resources

(c) extended rights of appeal for parents against an LEA's refusal to assess or reassess a child, against the contents of the statement, or an LEA's decision to cease to maintain a statement

(d) the establishment of the Special Educational Needs Tribunal, which replaced the local independent appeal committees and appeals to the Secretary of State.

While welcoming *The Parent's Charter* perspective which is implicit in these changes, many professionals are concerned about the 1993 Act's excessive concentration on the 2 or 3% of children who have statements. They believe that there is a lack of provision to help schools meet the needs of that much larger group of special needs children who do not have statements.

Evidence of the difficulties that schools are experiencing in their attempts to meet the needs of vulnerable children is reflected in the increasing number of requests for full assessment (often motivated at least in part by the resulting allocation of extra resources) and the increasing number of children excluded from school. Between 1990 and 1993 the proportion of pupils with a statement increased from 2.0% to 2.5%, despite the fact that most LEAs had policies intended to limit such an increase.

The official figures from the DFE's own two year research on permanent exclusions showed that 15% of the children excluded in the second year of the research were children with a statement: undoubtedly many of the others excluded were children with behavioural or learning difficulties.

The Code of Practice on the Identification and Assessment of Special Educational Needs

The **Education Act 1981** has been described as a charter for the 2% of children whose learning difficulties and disabilities required special provision and legally binding statements of SEN. When the **Education Act 1993** was being debated in both the House of Commons and Lords, there was considerable concern about whether this Act would advance the needs of the unstatemented 18% — those children who have SEN at some point in their school career, but who are not considered to require a statement under the 1981 Act.

Following these debates Baroness Blatch stressed that the Code would provide a full response to those who had been concerned that the 18% had been relatively neglected in the operation of the 1981 Act. The Code, which was published in April 1994, does require the school to look after the 18% and avoid what has been in some places an excessive tendency to rush to formal assessment and statementing.

Section 157 of the **Education Act 1993** gave a duty to the Secretary of State for Education to lay before Parliament a code of practice and regulations giving practical guidance to LEAs and all maintained schools on the discharge of their functions towards *all* children with special educational needs. The Code, which came into force in September 1994, is not legally binding but does have stronger force than a circular. In the words of the Minister, "any departure from the Code of Practice will, if challenged, require justification".

The SEN Tribunal, which has been set up under s.177 of the **Education Act 1993**, must have regard to any provisions of the Code which are relevant to the appeal. However, the tribunal adjudicates on individual cases and is not a regulatory body for schools.

Although the Code starts with the school-based assessment, this does not diminish the importance of addressing needs as early as possible, including the pre-school stage when appropriate. The emphasis on mainstream schools should also not diminish the relevance of the Code to special schools.

Principles, practices and procedures

The Code provides a coherent, clear and practically-based set of principles and guidance for schools in identifying and assessing SEN. It requires mainstream schools to follow a staged pattern of identification and assessment (similar to the Warnock stages and repeated in the 1992 Audit Commission report); establishes the role of the school SEN co-ordinator; and discusses the school's SEN policy which must be drawn up by the governors and reported annually to parents (s.161). It spells out clearly the practices and procedures which are essential to the principles of the Code:

- all children with SEN should be identified and assessed as early as possible and as quickly as is consistent with thoroughness

- provision for all children with SEN should be made by the most appropriate agency (in most cases this will be the child's mainstream school, working in partnership with the child's parents), no statutory assessment will be necessary
- where needed, LEAs must make assessments and statements in accordance with the prescribed time limits; must write clear and thorough statements setting out the child's educational and non-educational needs, the objectives to be secured, the provision to be made and the arrangements for monitoring and review; and ensure the annual review of the special educational provision arranged for the child and the updating and monitoring of educational targets
- special educational provision will be most effective when those responsible take into account the ascertainable wishes of the child concerned, considered in the light of his or her age and understanding
- there must be close co-operation between all the agencies concerned and a multi-disciplinary approach to the resolution of issues.

This list of practices and procedures, as with much of the Code, may read rather like a description of the good practice which many schools and LEAs are already following, but the Code will provide a clearer framework and clarify confusion about where responsibility lies.

Continuum of need and partnership

For the children discussed in this book, what is particularly important about the Code is that it recognises that there is a continuum of needs and provision and so it sets out the role of the school in relation to *all* pupils with special needs, including those who may not subsequently require a statement. Unlike the education legislation of the last decade, but in a similar manner to the **Children Act 1989**, it asserts that ascertaining the wishes of the child is essential for an effective assessment. It also reinforces the need for a partnership between parents, teachers, health workers, social workers and voluntary agencies.

In all these ways the practice described in the Code could be a blueprint for achieving more for the whole range of children with special needs.

The concerns are not so much about the principles it expresses, nor about the best way to proceed, but rather about the means by which to do so at a time of increasing demands on schools.

The focus in the Code on partnership between agencies working for the child is a particularly useful concept for schools. One of the most helpful messages for Heads when faced with children in need and unhappy children is that schools do not have to try to cope with everything on their own. There is to hand a powerful but sometimes underused resource in the access of energy, confidence and expertise which comes from getting all the agencies concerned with a child's welfare and development to work together with the school (Webb, 1989). Setting up a multi-agency support team can be one of the most effective ways of reinforcing the work of the school with these children. The team can give concrete help by:

(a) developing an integrated whole school policy for responding to the range of children with difficulties, and

(b) organising regular screening meetings to discuss, review and monitor particular children causing concern.

REFERENCES

Audit Commission, *Seen But Not Heard: Co-ordinating Community Child Health and Social Services for Children in Need*. HMSO, 1994.

DES, *The Children Act 1989: A Guide for the Education Service*. The Open University, 1991.

DES, Circular 22/89: *Assessments and Statements of Special Educational Needs: Procedures within the Education, Health and Social Services*. DES, 1989.

DFE, *Choice and Diversity: A New Framework for Schools*. Education White Paper. HMSO, 1992.

DFE/Welsh Office, *Code of Practice on the Identification and Assessment of Special Educational Needs*. DFE, 1994.

DoH, *The Children Act 1989 Guidance and Regulations: Vol 2 Family Support, Day Care and Educational Provision for Young Children.* HMSO, 1991.

DoH, *The Children Act 1989 Guidance and Regulations: Vol 6 Children With Disabilities.* HMSO, 1991A.

DoH, *The Children Act: A Guide for Parents.* DoH, 1991B.

Holman, B, *A New Deal for Social Welfare.* Lion, 1993.

Russell, P, *The Children Act 1989 and Disability,* Highlight No 109. National Children's Bureau, 1992.

Shaw, M, Masson, J, and Brocklesby, E, *Children in Need and Their Families: A New Approach.* University of Leicester/DoH, 1990.

Sinclair, R, *The Education of Children in Need: The Impact of Legislation,* Conference Lecture, Third Birmingham Childcare Conference. National Children's Bureau, 1994.

Webb, S, 'Interdisciplinary and Inter-agency Support' in Reid, K (ed), *Helping Troubled Pupils in Secondary Schools.* Blackwell, 1989.

Webb, S, 'Hunt is on for a New Esperanto', *TES,* 11.10.91.

SOURCES OF ADVICE, INFORMATION AND TRAINING

The following organisations may be useful sources of further information and advice. For addresses and information on the services available from these organisations please see chapter 9.

Council for Disabled Children
MENCAP
MIND
National Children's Bureau (NCB)
Young Minds

CHAPTER 7

WORKING IN PARTNERSHIP WITH PARENTS

WORKING WITH PARENTS

Special Educational Needs (The Warnock Report) (DES, 1978) argued that it is essential that parents are advised, encouraged and supported so that they can in turn effectively help their children.

The Hargreaves Report (ILEA, 1984) stated "If we want children to achieve more, especially working class children, then improved home-school liaison and increased parental involvement must be a top priority... parental commitment is a cornerstone of the school's success."

The Fish Report (ILEA, 1985) said "the recommendation for the development of an active partnership between schools, teachers and parents is central to our concern."

Choice and Diversity, the Education White Paper (DFE, 1992) stated that parental involvement is central to a good school ethos and one of the most significant factors in creating a good school is always going to be parental involvement in its life and progress.

Learning to Succeed, The National Commission on Education report (1993), argued that when schools fully exploit opportunities to involve parents in a productive way, parents, schools and children all gain.

Over the years, educational reports and policy documents have repeated the message that parental involvement and an active partnership between schools, teachers and parents is very important. Research findings have proved beyond question that parental involvement makes good educational sense. It helps to make educational opportunity more equal, raise achievement and increase parents' interest and confidence in the school. A number of studies have also shown that parents can make a major contribution to their children's learning through collaboration with teachers. This is true both in learning-to-read programmes and, for example, in developing personal competence in children with severe learning difficulties (Wolfendale, 1989).

The question is surely no longer whether this is the right thing to do, but rather *how* it is to be done. How can schools work towards an effective and dynamic partnership with parents and how can that partnership be extended to include those parents whose approach to school is apathetic or even downright antagonistic? Unsurprisingly, such parents are all too often the parents of the children who are the most troubled, the children who are causing havoc in class, or the children who seem withdrawn and stubbornly resistant to teachers' attempts to engage them.

A good relationship between school and home is important for *all* children, but for these children the quality of that relationship can be the crucial factor in educational achievement. Teachers who have a good relationship with parents will be more sensitive to home circumstances which may be affecting the child's progress, and have a better chance of responding at an early stage in a child's difficulties and providing a supportive and positive environment.

Before looking at strategies to improve home-school links, we need to remind ourselves of the changing nature of that relationship and the influence that education legislation has had on that change.

PARENTS' ATTITUDES AND THEIR NEW LEGAL RIGHTS

Parents' attitudes towards schools have undergone a sea change since the 1960s and 1970s: away from deference, puzzlement and helplessness and towards an understanding that they have a formal right to information and access concerning their children's schooling, and to a share in decisions regarding this (Jones, et al, 1992). Many parents are now truly active partners in education, and in many schools the traditional reluctances and inhibitions about parents being in school have faded.

Since 1980, education legislation has provided a steady increase in parental rights in such enactments as the following.

1. **Education Act 1980** — the rights to express a school preference, receive information about curriculum and organisation of the school, and increased representation on governing bodies.

2. **Education Act 1981** — the right to participate in assessment of special education needs (SEN) and the annual reviews, a right to information and to appeal (in each case within limits).

3. **Education (No 2) Act 1986** — annual reports and meetings for parents, increased representation on governing bodies.

4. **Education Reform Act 1988** — parental ballots on opting out, admission limits relaxed to allow open enrolment giving parents more chance to express preferences, the right to information on programme of work and progress.

5. **Education (Schools) Act 1992** — the right to consultation before formal inspection, the right to reports on individual children, including exam and test results.

6. **Education Act 1993** — independent tribunal to hear parents' appeals over children with SEN, Code of Practice for identification and assessment of SEN, rules governing school attendance and exclusion tightened up, new rules for opting out ballots.

The Parent's Charter (1991, updated 1994) reiterated what had been agreed through legislation, emphasised parents' rights to information on exam results, pupil attendance and staying-on rates.

Parental Choice

Speaking to the Centre for Policy Studies in April 1994, John Patten, then Secretary of State for Education, repeated again the Government's commitment to legislating for parental choice: "We have constantly emphasised the centrality of parental choice in our education reforms. It is built into the legislation governing the arrangements for grant-maintained status...parents decide." (*DFE News*, 95/94.)

What the law provides for is actually the right for parents to express a preference as to the school their child should attend. Expressing a preference is not, however, the same as exercising choice. In any case, what might loosely be called 'free market choice' in education creates winners and losers. The winners tend to be those parents who have the know-how and energy to push for the choice for their children and the losers are often those parents whose children have the greatest needs.

Michael Adler, in a report on Scotland's open enrolment experience, claimed that although there have been winners as well as losers, the gains achieved by some pupils have been fewer than the losses incurred by others and by the community as a whole (Adler, 1993).

Whatever the intentions or effects of education legislation, the reality in the day-to-day life of a school is that good home-school links transcend this conception of parents as consumers exercising legal rights. The HMI report, *Parents and Schools*, concluded that although it is for schools to decide how far they can or should invest in initiatives involving parents beyond what they are expected to provide in law, a robust partnership between home and school can bring worthwhile gains (HMI, 1991).

In a speech to the National Confederation of Parent Teacher Associations (NCPTA), Baroness Blatch, the former Minister of State at the DFE, compared the partnership to a marriage between parents and schools, in a sense an "arranged marriage. Like all good marriages, it needs to be worked at." (*DFE News*, 102/94)

Difficulties for Parents in the Home-school Partnership

Teachers know that not all parents will place the same value on education. Those parents, for instance, whose own experience of school was unhappy or unrewarding, may well be less than enthusiastic about the idea of working with the school. However, most parents, even those who initially appear apathetic or antagonistic want their children to have a decent education. What they may lack is an awareness of how important a contribution they can make to the educational process.

Strategies which will Help to Involve Parents

A parent's apparently hostile or 'not caring' attitude may, in reality, mask practical difficulties in attending meetings, social insecurity which makes them nervous about facing the Head or other teachers, or a defensiveness about their own 'failure' in the world of education. Care arrangements for small children (especially for single parents), working hours including shift work, and problems of language or literacy can all add to parents' difficulties in attending meetings or communicating with the school. Being aware of, and sensitive to, such possibilities and trying to help to find ways around them may not solve all the problems, but will create a more positive relationship on which to work. The following provides guidance for improving relationships.

1. Make sure that any written communication from school is friendly, clear and, if necessary, provided in languages other than English.

2. Provide a welcoming atmosphere for all who enter the school building: this might include a *Welcome to ... School* sign in the entrance, translated into any of the main community languages, and giving directions where visitors should go. However, it also should be considered whether using signs in the main community languages may make the users of other languages represented in the school feel even more excluded.

3. Have a room where parents can meet with other parents, with staff, or with the education welfare officer, who as well as offering welfare and other advice may help parents to arrange for speakers on subjects that interest them.

4. Adjust times of meetings with individual parents, if possible, to fit more easily with their work hours.

5. Involve parents as much as possible in the day-to-day life of the school.

6. Provide joint training or discussion groups for parents, teachers and members of the community.

7. Develop a home-school agreement in consultation with parents.

HOME-SCHOOL AGREEMENTS AND OTHER PROJECTS WITH PARENTS

A home-school agreement can be one of the most effective ways of creating an awareness of the parents' role in the educational process. It describes the particular responsibilities of parents in supporting the work of the school and the ways in which the school will help parents. As it is addressed to all parents (and should be drawn up in consultation with them), it can bring 'on board' some of the more reluctant participants. It can also increase parents' awareness that rights also imply responsibilities, such as encouraging good behaviour and good attendance, homework and reasonable bedtimes.

Setting up an agreement is a more complex operation than may first appear. In his practical guide to working with parents, John Bastiani explains that it evokes strong and widely-differing reactions (Bastiani, 1989). Planning and writing should be done in consultation with parents, pupils (where age makes this appropriate), governors, teachers, school support staff and local community organisations.

Calling it an agreement instead of a "contract" makes it sound less alarmingly formal and legal. DFE Circular 10/94, *Exclusions from School*, clarified this by noting that home-school agreements are useful but have no legal basis. They should not be included in the school's admission criteria and the breaking of an agreement is not in itself sufficient reason to exclude a pupil. Instead, the Head should consider whether the particular offence warrants exclusion, regardless of the agreement's existence (DFE, 1994).

The agreement needs to express clearly, in accessible and friendly language (including translations where needed), the responsibilities on the part of both the parent and the school. It can be a potent reciprocal learning experience, providing an opportunity for both partners to understand and respect each other's perspective and each other's role. If developed as part of a wider whole-school policy on parental partnership, it can become a useful yardstick against which to measure such a policy's success.

The Content of the Agreement

The specific content, style and wording require careful discussion to ensure that the agreement will match the ethos of the particular school and the needs and expectations expressed by the parents. Here, as a guide to areas which such an agreement might include, is a modified version of one which was developed in the London borough of Lewisham.

The parent agrees to:

- support and work with the school and encourage a positive attitude to education
- ensure that their child attends school regularly and punctually
- ensure that their child has a reasonable night's sleep before coming to school
- give time to talk and listen to their child, discuss homework when appropriate, and give positive support to efforts and progress the child has made
- attend meetings at school to discuss the child's progress and to learn about the work of the school

- let the school know if he or she has any concerns about the child's education

- let the school know if there are any factors which may affect the child's performance in school

- encourage the child to read and try to provide books and resources that will help with learning

- encourage the child to use the media, especially television, selectively, taking advantage of the programmes that help learning.

The school agrees to:

- provide a full and balanced curriculum and strive to educate each pupil to the best of his or her ability

- provide records and information about the child's educational progress, as well as the child's development in practical and social skills

- arrange regular meetings with the child's teacher(s) and be available at other times when the parent has concerns or questions

- send home examples of the child's work and books to read

- let the parent know immediately if his or her child is having any difficulties at school (in any discussion with parents this is always high on the list of their wishes)

- keep the parent informed about new policies and developments in school

- arrange facilities for parents to meet informally, eg a parents' room where space allows

- welcome all parents who wish to be part of any programmes for parents to help in the daily work of the school

- provide information about education benefits, where parents may go for help and advice and about the procedures for complaints.

In the end, the success of home-school agreements depends less on their form and content, than on the spirit in which they are approached and taken on board.

Working with Parents from Different Ethnic Groups

There are specific difficulties which families of ethnic minorities may face. For example, Asian parents have to negotiate the conflicts between bringing up their children as citizens of modern Britain and holding on to their traditional values and Afro-Caribbean families frequently face problems caused by racism and negative expectations from the police, and others in authority, or from bureaucracies public and private. For parents with English as a second language there is the additional hurdle of dealing with communication.

Undoubtedly, one of the most positive steps towards improvement in relationships would be an extensive programme of training, at initial and in-service levels, on the culture and expectations of different ethnic groups, which would increase awareness of the dangers of stereotyping pupils, parents and communities. The Commission for Racial Equality (CRE) may be able to provide some help with information materials. The other invaluable resource for teachers would be examples of good practice in some schools in areas such as Tower Hamlets, Lambeth, Kirklees and Bradford.

The OFSTED report on *Educational Support for Minority Ethnic Communities* underlined the vital importance of home-school links for tackling the underachievement of certain groups. OFSTED highlighted a project which established a forum for parents so that the school could hear their views; language classes for mothers; parent and toddler "stay and play" groups; and a number of schools who, with the help of their LEAs, had produced videos in the community languages about approaches to teaching reading, which explained educational terminology and aspects of the schools system. Schools involved in these projects recorded an increase in the confidence of parents and improvement in the behaviour and work of the pupils (OFSTED, 1994).

Parents with Literacy and Language Difficulties

Identifying parents who cannot read, and developing personal contact so that they can ask in confidence about the content of letters, may ease the intense sense of embarrassment that illiterate adults experience. The Adult Literacy and Basic Skills Unit recently claimed that one in eight young adults in Britain have problems with reading and writing and that a substantially larger number perform at a lower level than is required by the demands of everyday life and work. A useful source of help here might be the Manchester based National Elfrida Rathbone Society, which works with people with learning difficulties and literacy problems.

Home-school Liaison Projects and Training Materials

The HMI report, *Parents and Schools* (HMI, 1991), on the ways in which 32 primary schools and 38 secondary schools involved parents, describes a number of useful projects. In a school serving a new overspill estate with few amenities, for example, young mothers were encouraged to meet in a spare room. Suitable toys and educational activities were provided for the parents to play and work at with their young children. These early contacts carried through to the nursery and infant classes. In another example from a primary school on the edge of a large local authority housing estate, a corridor had been converted into a book area with comfortable seating. Mothers and fathers, given some advice on sharing books by teachers, came in throughout the day to read books with the pupils.

After a school reorganisation in 1988, Humberside, as part of an initiative to improve the quality of learning, appointed 42 primary home-school liaison (HSL) teachers with 50% non-teaching time. The number of teachers involved in the project with the University of Hull has grown to 60, and the majority of schools now pay for these posts through the compensatory element of their LMS budget which relates to socio-economic indicators.

Although the project began as a response to underachievement, and was therefore based on a compensatory model, stressing the importance of forging relationships with parents from less advantaged backgrounds, it became clear that this approach to education was needed in all schools. The project worked on a number of themes including:

(a) whole policy and its development

(b) 'unwilling' parents

(c) involving parents in specific aspects of their children's learning.

Evaluating Home-school Liaison Work

The detailed report, *Home School Liaison in Humberside: Teachers' Practices & Professional Expertise*, might make a useful starting point for any school considering adopting or reviewing a home-school policy. What makes it particularly useful is that the report describes a wealth of experience from Heads and teachers themselves (McNamara, et al, 1994).

In a similar way, the work of the University of Nottingham School of Education has been based on projects and debates with teachers over many years and John Bastiani's book, *Working with Parents* (1989), which came out of these studies, is full of practical and realistic suggestions for action.

There are many more sources of information for schools and training materials in this area. The National Association for Pastoral Care in Education (see chapter 9 for address), for example, has produced a set of workshop materials, *Developing Effective Links with Parents*, which shows how home-school links can be improved, and looks at factors and trends in contemporary family life. It also includes lists of teachers' complaints about parents and parents' complaints about teachers for discussion, which can loosen stereotypical views. A recently published training pack on *Tutoring* (from Longman Information and Reference, see chapter 9) gives practical advice on day-to-day relationships with parents, from writing personal letters to setting up tutor group parent meetings.

The Royal Society of Arts has provided some funding for advancing parental partnerships. One Head from a school in Lewisham, for example, said the project empowered home-school relationships and through it the school had been able to develop a course on ways of helping children with reading skills, establish a parents' newsletter, and start a joint course in calligraphy for parents, teachers and pupils.

Providing Joint Training/Discussion Groups for Teachers and Parents

One method of working and learning alongside parents might be through providing joint training sessions or evening workshops. There are many topics which affect the daily life of school and of home, and are of concern to both teachers and parents. These include:

(a) child development and behaviour at school and at home
(b) the influence of TV and the media on the behaviour and attitudes of children and young people
(c) the debate on moral and spiritual development
(d) drug and solvent abuse
(e) sex education, HIV and AIDS
(f) the different cultural and religious backgrounds of groups in the community.

Parents could be encouraged to make active contributions by providing some of the material, talking to the group about their experiences or simply by contributing to the discussions.

The Education Welfare Service (EWS)

At a recent national conference, Baroness Blatch reminded the audience of the valuable resource which the education welfare service (sometimes called the education social work service) provided as an important bridge between home, school and a range of other agencies such as the social services.

The Elton Report also emphasised the essential work of the service as a channel of communication between parents and school. If a pupil seems disturbed in school, the education welfare officer will often know the family and something of the difficulties which the child is experiencing. The service can support schools by:

(a) designing and negotiating home-school agreements with parents
(b) organising and running parents' rooms
(c) facilitating meetings for particular parents or for groups of parents in school, and

(d) supporting parents with children who are identified as having special needs, and helping them to understand the confusing detail of the assessment procedures and therefore feel confident enough to make their contribution to the process.

Parents in Partnership is a voluntary organisation which will give advice and support to parents of children with SEN.

OFSTED and the Changes in Parental Partnership

This chapter began by emphasising the particular importance of home-school links for children who are vulnerable and troubled. However, the **Education Reform Act 1988**, LMS, *The Parent's Charter*, and the statutory requirements to give information to parents and for the Office for Standards in Education (OFSTED) inspectors to meet with parents have resulted in a climate where effective relationships with all parents has become a central issue for schools.

Schedule 2 of the **Education (Schools) Act 1992** requires the authority for the school to arrange a meeting, between the registered inspector and those parents or registered pupils who wish to attend, where the parents' views are sought about the aspects of the school in the inspection schedule. The registered inspector will share the findings of the meeting with the Head and the chair of the governing body. The final inspection report will include an evaluation of the school's links with parents and their contribution to school life (OFSTED, 1993).

REFERENCES

Adler, M, *An Alternative Approach to Parental Choice*, Briefing No 13. National Commission on Education, 1993.

Bastiani, J, *Working with Parents: A Whole School Approach*. NFER-Nelson, 1989.

DES, *Special Educational Needs*, (The Warnock Report). HMSO, 1978.

DFE, *Choice and Diversity: A New Framework for Schools*, Education White Paper. HMSO, 1992.

DFE, Circular 10/94: *Exclusions from School*. DFE, 1994.

DFE, *The Parent's Charter*. DFE, 1991, updated 1994.

HMI, *Parents and Schools: Aspects of Parental Involvement in Primary and Secondary Schools*. DFE, 1991.

ILEA, *Improving Secondary Schools*, (The Hargreaves Report). Inner London Education Authority, 1984.

ILEA, *Education Opportunities for All?*, (The Fish Report). Inner London Education Authority, 1985.

Jones, G, et al, *A Willing Partnership*. Royal Society of Arts, 1992.

McNamara, D, et al, *Home School Liaison in Humberside: Teachers' Practices & Professional Expertise*. The University of Hull, 1994.

National Commission on Education, *Learning to Succeed*. Heinemann, 1993.

OFSTED, *Handbook for the Inspection of Schools*. HMSO, 1993.

OFSTED, *Educational Support for Minority Ethnic Communities*. OFSTED, 1994.

Wolfendale, S, *Parental Involvement*. Cassell, 1989.

SOURCES OF ADVICE, INFORMATION AND TRAINING

There are many organisations which can help parents. A number of these are discussed in the first chapter and listed at the end of that chapter. The following organisations may be useful sources of further information and advice. For addresses and information on the services available from these organisations please see chapter 9.

Commission for Racial Equality (CRE)

Longman Information and Reference

National Association for Pastoral Care in Education (NAPCE)

National Confederation of Parent-Teacher Associations (NCPTA)

National Elfrida Rathbone Association

Parents in Partnership (PIP)

CHAPTER 8

CHILDREN'S RIGHTS IN EDUCATION

CHILDREN'S RIGHTS

It was not until the early part of this century that children's rights to justice were formally and internationally recognised. The League of Nations adopted the Declaration of the Rights of the Child in 1924, followed by the United Nations Declaration in 1959 and 30 years later the UN Convention on the Rights of the Child. In 1991, our Government ratified the Convention. There are now 154 countries which have ratified the Convention and each country is monitored for its compliance with the Convention's articles.

The area in which education legislation and policy is lagging behind most seriously is in relation to Article 12, which is the heart of the Convention. It gives the child: "who is capable of forming his or her own views the right to express those views freely in all matters affecting the child, the views of the child being given due weight in accordance with the age and maturity of the child".

Our education legislation, however, including the **Education Act 1993**, is lacking any legal requirement for children to be consulted about decisions made on their behalf. Ironically, the only pupils who have a legal right to have their views considered are pupils *out* of school and the subject of an education supervision order, because these orders come under the **Children Act 1989**. However, because a legal right is wider than a statutory right, it could be argued that children with special educational needs do now have a legal right to be consulted under the Code of Practice.

Lord Elton tabled an amendment to the Education Bill which became the **Education Act 1993** calling on governing bodies and LEAs to use their best endeavours to secure that:

(a) on any matter which affects a pupil the views of the pupil are given due consideration

(b) steps are taken to ascertain these views, and

(c) pupils are provided with the opportunity to be heard in any administrative proceeding which affects them.

There was particular concern about the need for this amendment because Allan Levy QC had found that the "Children Act 1989 does not provide for Article 12 to have effect in respect of any of the relevant education matters" (Hansard, 21.6.93). In spite of this advice the amendment was withdrawn.

The Children Act 1989, Education Legislation and the Code of Practice

The focus on parental wishes in Education Acts is clearly stated regarding such matters as choice of school in ordinary circumstances and references to religious denomination which strictly relate to that of the parent and not specifically of the child. The special educational needs Code of Practice does, however, nod in the direction of Children Act philosophy when advising that children's views be taken into account. The Code states that children have a right to be heard and schools should consider how they:

(a) involve pupils in decision-making processes

(b) determine the pupil's level of participation, taking into account approaches to assessment and intervention which are suitable for his or her age

(c) record pupils' views when identifying their difficulties, setting goals and monitoring progress

(d) involve pupils in implementing individual education plans.

The UK Agenda for Children

The Children's Rights Development Unit (CRDU) has worked collaboratively with a wide range of organisations and consulted children and young people to produce a *UK Agenda for Children* to be submitted to the UN Committee (CRDU, 1994). This provides a systematic analysis of the extent to which law, policy and practice in education and other fields complies, or fails to comply, with the standards of the UN Convention.

With this document Heads will be able to assess their school's performance on ensuring the rights of children on a wide range of issues, from admission procedures and exclusions to English as a second language and bullying. Peter Newell's book, *The UN Convention and Children's Rights in the UK*, gives a good background study of the education implications of the Convention and includes the complete text (Newell, 1991).

The Agenda points out that in order to be effective, multicultural education must take place in the context of an active commitment to anti-racism. National Curriculum Council (NCC) guidance is lacking in clarity about the use and meaning of the terms 'equal opportunities' and 'minority ethnic groups' and makes no reference to racism. According to the Chair of the Advisory Centre for Education (ACE), multicultural issues are being excluded from the National Curriculum when it is increasingly important to encourage young people to understand and value ethnic diversity (Tomlinson, 1993). The Commission for Racial Equality (CRE) has called for a legislative framework for multicultural education.

Equality, Rights and Racism

Black and Asian children are frequently disadvantaged before they arrive in school. Statistics show that they are more likely to be living in families where parents are unemployed, struggling with financial hardship or poor housing conditions. Such conditions may be further compounded by experiences of racism in the community or in the school, or by being excluded from school. The DFE's research on exclusion statistics over two years revealed that over 8% of the children excluded were Afro-Caribbean, which is four times their proportion in the school population (DFE, 1992).

Newham authority, with the second highest reported racial assaults figures in England, has established an anti-racial harassment policy for its schools. Heads will find a video and trainers book, *Painful Lessons*, describing how the Newham schools have addressed racism, useful when working on a policy for their own schools (BBC Education, 1993 — see chapter 9). One technique described in the video involves using young people to talk individually to pupils who have been subjected to racism or who are racially harassing others. A number of schools in other parts of the country have used such peer group counselling to address the problem of bullying.

Improving Motivation and Self-respect

Creating a school environment in which children are listened to and respected can and does reinforce pupils' self-respect and motivation to learn. This is particularly important for pupils who have to cope with extra difficulties or are distressed by problems at home. Some children may be lower achievers because their destructive emotions — fear, anger, extreme sadness — are sapping their motivation to work. Others may falter because they lack the intellectual ability to make progress: often both factors apply, and compound each other.

Learning programmes that support achievement and encourage pupils to try again are clearly the most effective way in which schools can nurture a child's self-respect. A positive sense of self-esteem cannot alter innate ability, but it will help children to achieve and to survive the effects of failure, hardship and stress in their lives.

Consulting Children and Providing Boundaries

To regret the fact that education legislation has not installed legal require-ments to consult children is not, of course, to encourage abdication of responsible authority on the part of Heads and teachers. Neither the **Children Act 1989** nor the Convention implies that children's views will always be right, or that we should treat them as if they were adults, giving them the responsibility of making complex and difficult decisions. This would be intrinsically unfair and would take away from them the security of parental and adult authority which is, after all, another of their rights.

THE ROLE OF THE SCHOOL — RIGHTS AND RESPONSIBILITIES

Heads need to ask what can be done in schools both to ensure that children are given their rights and to encourage them to grow into mature and caring citizens.

The Government has been concerned that schools should do as much as possible to promote the spiritual and moral development of pupils and it has, in DFE Circular 1/94, *Religious Education and Collective Worship*, recently required schools to include a statement of ethos in their prospec-tus.

However, writing down a set of shared values is only the beginning. What is moral intelligence, and how is it to be taught? It is clearly not as simple as learning a rote list of dos and don'ts — what the NCC discus-sion paper on *Spiritual and Moral Development* (1993) calls values which contain moral absolutes.

Pupils come into schools with views which reflect the values of their parents and their peer groups on the dilemmas of everyday life in the late twentieth century, from shoplifting to truancy and the use of drugs. Studies of delinquent adolescents do not suggest a lack of moral awareness among the youngsters, but rather an alienation from mainstream expectations. The crux of the matter for schools, therefore, is how to help and motivate pupils to resist competing pressures, and to accept that the rules apply to them.

One way is to use the curriculum for developing thinking and debate. Mary Midgely, a philosopher who has been writing in this field for some years, believes that only through serious thinking exercised in serious discussion will schools be able "to relieve the stress of confusion in a changing, pluralistic society". Discussion of this kind can be carried on in schools with quite young children, but it involves treating their views with a new kind of respect.

The OFSTED *Handbook for the Inspection of Schools* suggests that evidence of schools' ability to promote their pupils' personal development will include whether the quality of relationships is such that pupils feel free to express and explore their views openly and honestly, and are willing to listen to opinions which they may not share (OFSTED, 1993).

As well as Mary Midgeley's books, Heads may find John White's *Education and the Good Life* a useful discussion on 'moral development' as an educational aim (White, 1990).

School Strategies for Respecting Rights and Encouraging Social Responsibility

Strategies to ensure that children are given their rights *and* encouraged to grow into responsible citizens might include the following.

1. A corporate whole-school approach to behaviour which views discipline as a positive phenomenon — not just a matter of restraint, control and punishment — and concentrates on the quality of human relationships throughout the school. Good relationships between pupils, and

between pupils and teachers, thus become an integral part of the culture of the school, encouraging a shared sense of responsibility for standards of behaviour.

2. A joint undertaking on the part of all adults in the school to listen to, and treat with respect, the views of pupils. Adolescents frequently complain that they feel they are not given the opportunity to express their views, and that adults do not take them seriously or dismiss them as immature. It is only through being valued themselves, however, that children learn to value others.

3. Opportunities for pupils to take on responsibility giving them experience in decision making. This might be done by actively involving pupils in their own assessment through Records of Achievement (RoA) or through such forums as school councils to discuss and decide on school policies for behaviour and bullying. Promoting the right to be heard and be part of a democratic process is probably the most powerful lesson the school can provide on growing up as citizens in a democracy.

4. Using the curriculum to help pupils to come to grips with the complex nature of the inter-relationships between rights and social responsibility in our society. The NCC discussion paper, although bland in parts, might be a starting point (NCC, 1993). A much more immediate and useful connection to their world, however, could be made through debates on the sort of messages which are presented to them by TV and the media.

REFERENCES

CRDU, *UK Agenda for Children*. Children's Rights Development Unit, 1994.

DFE, *Exclusions: A Discussion Paper*. DFE, 1992.

DFE, Circular 1/94: *Religious Education and Collective Worship*. DFE, 1994.

NCC, *Spiritual and Moral Development*. Information Team, NCC, 1993.

Newell, P, *The UN Convention and Children's Rights in the UK*. National Children's Bureau, 1991.

OFSTED, *Handbook for the Inspection of Schools*. HMSO, 1993.

Tomlinson, S, 'A Nationalistic Curriculum for White Superiority?' in *ACE Bulletin*, No 51, 1993.

White, J, *Education and the Good Life*. Kogan Page, 1990.

SOURCES OF ADVICE, INFORMATION AND TRAINING

The following organisations may be a useful source of further information and advice. For addresses and information on the services available from these organisations please see chapter 9.

BBC Education Mosaic

Children's Legal Centre

Children's Rights Development Unit (CRDU)

Commission for Racial Equality (CRE)

CHAPTER 9

SOURCES OF ADVICE, INFORMATION AND TRAINING

ADVISORY CENTRE FOR EDUCATION (ACE)
1B Aberdeen Studios
22 Highbury Grove
London N5 2EA
Tel: 0171-354 8321

ACE is an independent national advice centre offering advice on any aspect of the State education system. Publications include information handbooks and a magazine for parents. The advice line is open on weekdays from 2pm to 5pm.

ASIAN FAMILY COUNSELLING SERVICE
74 The Avenue
London W13 8LB
Tel: 0181-997 5749

This service provides marital counselling services — meditation, counselling and training — for Asian families.

BBC EDUCATION MOSAIC
PO Box 50
Wetherby
West Yorkshire
LS23 7E2
Tel: 01937 541001

BBC Education Mosaic has produced *Painful Lessons*, a video and book about racism for trainers which is available from BBC Education Developments.

CHAR (HOUSING CAMPAIGN FOR SINGLE PEOPLE)
5–15 Cromer Street
London WC1 8LS
Tel: 0171-833 2071

CHAR consists of a number of voluntary groups which give housing advice to 16- to 17-year-olds.

CHILDLINE
Freepost 1111
London N1 0BR
Tel: 0800 1111

Childline is a 24 hour national freephone counselling service for children in trouble or danger.

CHILD POVERTY ACTION GROUP
4th Floor
1–5 Bath Street
London EC1V 9PY
Tel: 0171-253 3406

The Child Poverty Action Group gives advice and provides an advocacy service on welfare rights via advice workers from branches throughout the country. It also provides courses and publications.

CHILDREN'S LEGAL CENTRE

20 Compton Terrace
London N1 2UN
Tel: 0171-359 9392, Advice line: 0171-359 6251 (open 2pm to 5pm)

The centre is an independent national organisation which gives advice on law and policy by telephone and letter. It publishes a monthly magazine, *Childright*.

CHILDREN'S RIGHTS DEVELOPMENT UNIT (CRDU)

235 Shaftesbury Avenue
London WC2H 8EL
Tel: 0171-240 4449

THE CHILDREN'S SOCIETY

Edward Rudolf House
69–85 Margery Street
London WC1X 0JL
Tel: 0171-837 4299

This is a national childcare organisation offering advice for children, young people and families. It runs family centres, works with young people living on the streets and with children with disabilities. The society also publishes educational material for schools and story books for children.

CHILDWATCH

206 Hessle Road
Hull
North Humberside HU3 3BE
Tel: 01482 25552

Childwatch is an education and child abuse prevention unit. It publishes information for teachers and parents and provides a counselling service.

113

CITIZENS ADVICE BUREAUX (CAB)

The CAB gives free, confidential and impartial advice on legal and general subjects including housing and parental rights (branches are listed in local telephone directories). They also publish information and use the experience of clients' problems to suggest improvements to local social policy and services.

COMMISSION FOR RACIAL EQUALITY (CRE)
10–12 Allington Street
London SW1E 5EH
Tel: 0171-828 7022

The Commission institutes proceedings in cases of racial discrimination. Publications include information leaflets, some of which are available in Asian languages.

CONTACT-A-FAMILY
170 Tottenham Court Road
London W1P 0HA
Tel: 0171-383 3555
This organisation provides a network of support groups for parents of children with disabilities or special needs. It also provides information and publications.

COUNCIL FOR DISABLED CHILDREN
8 Wakley Street
London EC1V 7QE
Tel: 0171-843 6000
The Council was formerly the Voluntary Council for Handicapped Children. It is a multidisciplinary council which provides information and advice and promotes parental involvement in assessment. It also assists people in developing information material for their peers and with decision making.

CRUSE
126 Sheen Road
Richmond
Surrey TW9 1UR
Tel: 0181-940 4818
Helpline: 0181-332 7227

CRUSE provides help for bereaved children and adults through 194 local branches. Training packs, including *Supporting Bereaved Children and Families*, books and leaflets are available.

DEVON TRAVELLER EDUCATION SERVICE
Civic Centre
Plymouth PL1 2EW
Tel: 01752 385509

This service has produced the *Between Two Worlds* video and booklets for schools.

DRUG HELPLINE

The helpline provides a 24 hour service for local help with drug problems. Dial 100, ask for Freephone Drug Problems and you will be given a number for each of the 14 regions in England.

EUROPEAN FEDERATION FOR THE EDUCATION OF THE CHILDREN OF OCCUPATIONAL TRAVELLERS (EFECOT)
Rue de l'Industrie
42/10 B-1040
Brussels
Belgium

EXPLORING PARENTHOOD
Latimer Education Centre
194 Freston Road
London W10 6TT
Tel: 0181-960 1678 (10am to 4pm, weekdays)

Exploring Parenthood gives professional support, advice and counselling to parents. The organisation also publishes information leaflets, including leaflets on drugs and solvents, and offers workshops and groupwork for schools.

FAMILY SERVICE UNIT
207 Marylebone Road
London NW1 5QP
Tel: 0171-402 5175

This is a national organisation which promotes the welfare of severely disadvantaged families through social work intervention. Provision includes playschemes, material help, advice and counselling.

FAMILY WELFARE ASSOCIATION
501–505 Kingsland Road
London E8 4AU
Tel: 0171-254 6251

The association assists families to overcome the effects of poverty by providing practical, emotional and financial support.

GINGERBREAD
49 Wellington Street
London WC2E 7BN
Adviceline: 0171-240 0953

This is a national organisation with 500 UK suport groups for lone-parents and their children and publications on benefits and rights.

HEALTHWISE LTD
9 Slater Street
Liverpool L1 4BW
Tel: 0151-707 2262

This organisation produces training packs, including *Don't Panic*, for secondary schools, dealing with confidentiality, contacting the police, etc.

HOME START UK
2 Salisbury Road
Leicester LE2 7QR
Tel: 0116-255 4988
Home Start UK volunteers offer friendship and practical help to families under stress to help to prevent family breakdown.

INSTITUTE FOR THE STUDY OF DRUG DEPENDENCE
Waterbridge House
32–36 Loman Street
London SE1 0EE
Tel: 0171-928 1211
The Institute produces a wide range of leaflets, including *So you've chosen 'drugs' for your project?*, which gives information for secondary school pupils doing projects on drugs. There is also a comprehensive library (tel: 0171-928 7071).

LIFELINE PROJECT
Globe House
Southall Street
Manchester M3 1LG
Tel: 0161-834 7160

Lifeline is a North West drug training unit and provides materials and training. Training can be 'tailor made' to adapt to particular needs.

LONGMAN INFORMATION AND REFERENCE
Westgate House
Harlow
Essex CM20 1YR
Tel: 01279 442601

The Longman Group produces training materials, including Eve Brock's *Child Abuse & the School's Response* and C Watkins and J Thackers' *Tutoring: INSET Workshops for a Whole School Approach*.

MEDICAL FOUNDATION FOR THE CARE OF VICTIMS OF TORTURE
96–98 Grafton Road
Kentish Town
London NW5 3EJ
Tel: 0171-284 4321

The foundation supports survivors of torture and their families and also provides training and information.

MENCAP
123 Golden Lane
London EC1Y 0RT
Tel: 0171-454 0454

MENCAP provides advice for people with learning difficulties and their families. It also provides training.

MIND
Granta House
15 Broadway
Stratford
E15 4BQ
Tel: 0181-519 2122

MIND consists of 230 local associations providing counselling, housing projects, etc, for people with mental health problems.

THE MINORITY RIGHTS GROUP
379 Brixton Road
London SW9 7DE
Tel: 0171-978 9498

This group provides publications on minority groups, including refugees and the conflicts they have fled, and useful education materials for teachers.

NATIONAL ASSOCIATION FOR PASTORAL CARE IN EDUCATION (NAPCE)

Education Department
University of Warwick
Coventry CV4 7AL
Tel: 01203 523523

NAPCE provides publications, conferences and training materials including P Wagner (1993) *Children and Bereavement, Death and Loss: What Can the School Do?*

NATIONAL ASSOCIATION OF TEACHERS OF TRAVELLERS (NATT)

Graiseley Centre
Pool Street
Wolverhampton
West Midlands
WV2 4NE
Tel: 01902 714646

NATIONAL CHILDREN'S BUREAU (NCB)

8 Wakley Street
London EC1V 7RE
Tel: 0171-843 6000

The NCB conducts research and provides conferences, training packs and various publications including over 100 information sheets on bereavement, SEN, family breakdown, children in care, solvent misuse, etc.

NATIONAL CONFEDERATION OF PARENT TEACHER ASSOCIATIONS (NCPTA)

2 Ebbsleet Estate
Stonebridge Road
Gravesend
Kent DA11 9DZ
Tel: 01474 560618

Many branches of this association offer advice to members on educational matters and publish a magazine and news-sheet.

NATIONAL COUNCIL FOR ONE PARENT FAMILIES
255 Kentish Town Road
London NW5 2LX
Tel: 0171-267 1361

This organisation provides counselling, information and legal advice for lone-parents.

NATIONAL ELFRIDA RATHBONE ASSOCIATION
Head Office
1st Floor
The Excalibur Building
77 Whitworth Street
Manchester M1 6EZ
Tel: 0161-236 5358

The association creates opportunities for children and adults with learning difficulties, providing education sessions, playgroups, holiday schemes, etc. Some projects are run in other parts of the country.

NATIONAL SOCIETY FOR THE PREVENTION OF CRUELTY TO CHILDREN (NSPCC)
42 Curtain Road
London EC2A 3MH
Tel: 0171-825 2500

The NSPCC has many local branches which investigate reports of ill treatment, offer advice and training and provide family centres and other preventive projects.

NATIONAL STEPFAMILY ASSOCIATION
72 Willesden Lane
London NW6 7TA
Tel: 0171-372 0844

The association provides advice and information to members of stepfamilies and those who work with them.

NCH ACTION FOR CHILDREN
85 Highbury Park
London N5 1UD
Tel: 0171-226 2033

NCH has over 100 family centres and a nationwide network of specialist treatment centres providing therapy for sexually abused children and for non-abusing family members. Projects for disability and homelessness.

THE OPEN UNIVERSITY
Walton Hall
Milton Keynes MK7 6AA
Tel: 01908 653743

The Open University has published an extensive and detailed training pack on the **Children Act 1989**, *P558 The Children Act 1989: Putting it into Practice* (1991), which may be purchased in separate sections. The *Reference Pack*, containing 23 summary cards on parental responsibility, court orders etc, is probably the most useful for teachers. There is also a video of illustrative cases included in the *Trainers' Pack*.

PARENTLINE
Westbury House
57 Hart Road
Thundersley
Essex SS7 3PD
Helpline: 01268 757077

Parentline gives support to parents under stress, therefore maximising a family's capacity to care for its children.

PARENTS IN PARTNERSHIP (PIP)
Portacabin
Clare House
Blackshaw Road
SW17 0QT
Tel: 0171-735 7735

PIP gives information and advice to parents of children with SEN and offers support during assessments of their children.

RAINBOWS FOR ALL CHILDREN
Leeds Diocesan RE Centre
62 Headingley Lane
Leeds LS6 2BU
Tel: 0113-274 0344

This organisation runs programmes for children who have experienced parental death or separation.

THE REFUGEE COUNCIL
3–9 Bondway House
Bondway
Vauxhall
London SW8 1SJ
Tel: 0171-582 6922

The Refugee Council provides training for schools, practical advice for refugees and refugee advisors and a useful booklet, *Refugees in the Class-room*.

RELATE MARRIAGE GUIDANCE
Herbert Gray College
Little Church Street
Rugby CV21 3AP
Tel: 01788 573241

Relate is a national network of marital counsellors who help over 70,000 couples each year. The association also provides literature and information.

RELEASE
388 Old Street
London EC1V 9LT
Tel: 0171-729 5255

Release specialises in drugs and the law, offering advice, training and publications. The helpline will give advice to teachers when pupils are found with drugs. (The helpline telephone is: daytime — 0171-729 9904; overnight — 0171-603 8654.)

RE-SOLV
30A High Street
Stone
Staffordshire
ST15 8AW
Tel: 01785 817885

RE-SOLV provides training materials and videos on solvent and volatile substance abuse for teachers and parents.

SHELTER
88 Old Street
London EC1V 9HU
Tel: 0171-253 0202

Shelter gives advice to homeless people and practical help through a national network of 29 centres and provides emergency shelter in London.

THE ADVISORY COUNCIL ON ALCOHOL AND DRUG EDUCA-TION (TACADE)
1 Hulme Place
The Crescent
Salford
Manchester M5 4QA
Tel: 0161-745 8925

TACADE provides training materials and courses on aspects of personal and social education as well as drugs, including *Skills for the Primary School Child: Promoting the Protection of Children.*

TRAINING ADVISORY GROUP (TAG)
c/o Jenny Price
76 Nutgrove Road
St. Helens
WA9 5TL

TAG is a joint DFE and education social work association group which provides advice, training and training materials on aspects of attendance, working with parents, special needs and child employment.

WOMEN'S AID FEDERATION ENGLAND (WAFE)
PO Box 391
Bristol
BS99 7WS
Tel: 0117-963 3494
Helpline: 0117-942 1392

The association provides help for women experiencing physical, emotional and sexual violence and provides emergency accommodation, advice and support.

YOUNG MINDS
22A Boston Place
London NW1 6ER
Tel: 0171-724 7262
Helpline: 0345 626376

Young Minds is a national voluntary organisation working to promote the mental health of children, young people and their families and to increase awareness of the effects of different forms of violence on the mental health of children. It offers advice, publications and seminars.

INDEX